THINKING
ON THE OTHER SIDE
OF ZERO
PART 2

D1637943

THINKING
ON THE OTHER SIDE
OF ZERO
PART 2

ALAN JOSEPH OLIVER

Library of Congress Control Number:		2022907740
ISBN:	Hardcover	978-1-6698-8855-0
	Softcover	978-1-6698-8854-3
	eBook	978-1-6698-8853-6

Print information available on the last page.

Rev. date: 11/10/2022

To order additional copies of this book, contact:
Xlibris
AU TFN: 1 800 844 927 (Toll Free inside Australia)
AU Local: (02) 8310 8187 (+61 2 8310 8187 from outside Australia)
www.Xlibris.com.au
Orders@Xlibris.com.au
839577

CONTENTS

FOREWORD

The human organism tends to think out problems along two general descriptive lines; the situation as it is, as might occur in a photograph and the same situation developed by syllogism or analysis; A leads to B leads to C and so forth. Terms applied to these logic systems are respectively intuitive or deductive. In general terms, science extensively uses the latter and it is undoubted that science owes its appeal over the past three or four centuries to a remarkable success for the material components of those same human organisms. For the science practitioners, this success has carried with it quite gratuitously, implicitly, or explicitly, the axiom: if the system is not available to an approach via the syllogism, which usually means that A, B and C are real or material, it cannot exist or be worthy of the scientific approach. In a Cartesian paraphrase, "I exist therefore I am", the insular isolation is not in doubt.

Different civilisations of these organisms have embraced different belief systems, a circumstance in which it is possible to shear on rather philosophical lines the intuiters and the deducers. Recent civilisations, for example the Oriental, the Egyptian and the Mayan before them, tend to follow the intuitive. On the other hand, the Greco-Roman civilisations whence originated the bulk of the scientific method as we know it, were more embracing of the deductive than the intuitive and this has meant, again rather gratuitously, that these civilisations and the science which followed them has little heed for the unreal, amounting in many cases to a frank disdain. A celebrated practitioner of more recent times was Albert Einstein, who epitomised the system for physicists (the discipline charged by that civilisation with knowing about things) by advising that if it is not real then it is not physics, inferring that any other system was best left to the sport of musing such as mathematics. There were oppressive penalties in the club for abjuring these principles.

Granted that all the human organisms of all time have yearned for notions of origin and destiny, the intuiters have tended to reside these eternal queries in the unreal which the Greco-Roman based science would locate in dimensions above three, where the deducers are obliged to gainsay or otherwise ignore the extra dimensional (beyond three) as misgiving and mischievous.

Within the seeming discreteness of the two logic systems there have arisen many scholarly treatises seeking their reconciliation or assimilation in a more comprehensive analysis of the nature of existence and its direction. Alan Oliver is one of the more recent of these, where his insight has sought to meld the two systems by probes that go back in review, some thousands of years in the case of the intuiters and to the bases of Greece and Rome in the case of the deducers. With the inexorability of water dripping on a rock, this work will join the others celebrated in their attempts to ask reason to prevail, sanctioned only by the evidence. I am one of the few more pessimistic practitioners of the Greco-Roman science who seized the honour of the opportunity of writing this book's Foreword to derive the reason for a pessimism in an attempt to explain abject disbelief, the frustration coupled with the ingrained reticence that the author's logic involves toward a recognition of what is clear to many of us, the obvious. I cannot believe that we can ascribe this manifest profound ingraining to simple prejudice. Its hold on reason is far too strong for that. It would be more valuable were there a more acceptable (possibly science-based) reason for this profound tenure. I therefore seized on the Foreword to present one prejudice free viewpoint.

Some mathematicians have recently pondered the aversion of Western thinking to the use of zero and beyond, a term that they have long used in their formalism. In so doing they research its origins in Western writings. One report for instance concerned a bookmaker's clerk who used i (as the square root of minus one, often used to indicate a progression into dimensions beyond the usual three), to assess the odds for his master's next appearance at the Hippodrome with a time circa 1490 AD.

If we delve for a moment into the proposed mechanism wherein behaviour emerges into a species performance, we choose the fruit fly, with a generation every several hours or so. Roughly three thousand generations are needed for a behavioural imprint to take hold or to become a trait in a mechanism which we could liken to the establishment in the brain of a critical mass for thinking about that trait. If we use a figure of circa thirty years for the expiry of one human generation, this means circa fifteen generations have elapsed since this early first use of i, certainly well below the fruit fly as a fixation time required for the aforementioned critical mass. This idea asserts that little grasp of the supradimensional is in early prospect. The contra argument will be that the learning curve of an insect will be far slower than that of a human, but I wonder!

Meanwhile there must be considerable scope for manuscripts of the Oliver type which present the argument bereft of any semblance of the evangelical overlay sometimes found in the logic of authors in the field. The facts are laid bare for the reader, and they involve a recherché so necessary to counter the sheer imminence of materialist Western thought. The burgeoning literature in reference to this imbalance is of topical interest for the confrontation of cultures that have continued to permeate these two cultures, the intuitive and the deductive. Scholars can continue to take advantage of the appearance of a further careful reasoning of the Oliver stance on this omnipresent and omniscient issue.

Science is replete with evanescent ideas and, if by good fortune the 3000-generation fixation idea could be truncated to 3 generations so that scientists now applied their deductive mode to the supradimensional, the outcome might be prodigious of the type seen for the material world over the last few centuries. It needs only the grasp that spacetime is nearly as manipulable as its derivatives in the real energy world of Faraday for which, anyhow, space is really the seed catalyst. Indeed, the same grasp can see the mystique of the space worlds succumb to a building block manipulable form that is the success story of their strict counterparts in the real world. Perhaps as an overstatement, all of the catalysis of spacetime energy underpins in an insidious fashion, all of the anthropomorphism of the advances of the past three or four centuries.

The cliché, "theory of everything", is increasingly applied to the analogy of this metamorphosis, and may betoken the welcome truncation I have referred to. We could, in this context, quickly anticipate the use of the free energy of Schauberger's nostra to assist with the reversal of much of the disease process by the sheer logic involved with Boolean formalism and its inversion, so welcome in its rationality amidst the avalanche of therapeutic chemicals. We could anticipate the restoration of water supply to the pristine state of yesteryear, a copy of the metabolism of the tree or shrub outside the window, which has fixed a kilogram of sugar as you read this, a list which is interminable toward bonhomie and well-being consonant with the emergence of a grasp, possible crumb by crumb in human progress derivable from authors of Oliver's encouragement.

Herewith the seeds of renaissance.
Bevan L Reid,
MD. Dip. TM&H. BVSc. Late Faculty of Medicine,
University of Sydney. 2005.

INTRODUCTION

Why Part 2?

I am writing *"Thinking on the Other Side of Zero²*, Part 2, to answer the questions arising from *"Thinking on the Other Side of Zero¹*, Part 1. I am aware of the questions a reader might have about the yoga state of Samadhi, from The Yoga Sutras of Patanjali, Samadhi Pada, Volume1³, (authored by Pandit Usharbuddh Arya, who became Swami Veda Bharati). I don't think my diagrams of the process of consciousness, used at the end of Part 1, are sufficient to understand that fundamental process, for the simple reason that I didn't understand the process at the time.

I can honestly say I can't ignore this process of consciousness and the questions it raises in me. Now, with the benefit of an aspect of that process (hindsight), I need to begin by saying that what I want to explain are the relevant yoga sutras in terms of recognised physics by recognised physicists, while providing the physics (suggested by GS Srinivasan in Sankhya Karika⁴) in the Yoga Sutras to better explain what each has in common with the other. I will acknowledge them in the References section at the end of this book.

In my view, the best way to explain being in that Samadhi state would be to combine my secondary school physics with the science inferred in The Yoga Sutras of Patanjali, and in the more detailed science in "Sankhya Karika⁴," by G. Srinivasan.

In *"Thinking on the Other Side of Zero*[1], Part 1, I had mentioned some of the healing sessions I had with people who had sought my help, and from the perspective of Bohm's Wholeness and the Implicate Order[5]. I will employ that same science to describe the healing experienced by my subjects. I am ready to explain being 'accidentally' in that state, but first, some of my background by way of introduction.

I began the first iteration of this book, which I self-published in 1983, as "A Free Fall into Unstructured Thinking[6]." I had hoped to find a way to understand how I think because I knew the people around me thought my process of thinking was weird, illogical, or simply irritating at best, and they would ask for an explanation of why and how I arrived at my answer to their question. This intrigued me because I thought the answer was obvious; at least it was to me, doesn't everyone think this way?

The more I thought about thinking as mentally processing information, the more difficult it became to find anything at all because empty is the normal state of my mind. As an experiment, I would think of a word or a situation, and write whatever thoughts came to mind. From there, I thought of consciousness as three steps in an uncomplicated process; it was my awareness of information in one moment of relatedness; which related to a new thought, question, or idea; with the answer following as the next thought. This process left me to wonder where the answer came from.

Then one night during a break in an Est[7] seminar in 1983, a young woman asked me if we could meet for coffee and a quiet talk after the seminar. She said she had noticed I was calm, and she needed advice on personal issues. That young woman was Emma Gray, a part-time actor/singer and office worker who became a friend in need of support at a challenging time in her life, and Est didn't provide the answers she needed.

Our talks became counselling for Emma, and I made notes about our sessions in what ended up as the beginning of this book, version 1, in 1984. In that first book, I described some of my experiences as a healer, experiences which raised questions about reality and mind, all of which were included in my first book, "A Free Fall into Unstructured Thinking[6]."

The second iteration of the book, "Thinkerman, and the Accident of Knowing[8]," was a simple record of my reflections on my experiences in Samapatti, and how they might be seen in relation to some of my conversations with the people who were the subjects of those experiences. It was really a way to stay connected with what I had learned from my mentor, Dr Bevan Reid, who had moved interstate and for a long time we lost touch.

By then I had moved to Queensland with my wife Cecily, whom I married in 1992. Cecily had visions of recreating a small hobby farm to replicate the happy times in her former marriage, but her son had become estranged from her and that had hurt her deeply.

After five years on our 40-acre hobby farm, with Cecily still depressed and none of her family visiting, I had a double bypass operation which made the work on the farm too difficult for me. We sold the farm and moved to Port Elliot in South Australia, where Cecily hoped being closer to her children might help resolve the issues with her family. Her son and his family remained resolutely apart from Cecily, but her two daughters, Fiona and Gabrielle, and their families were now in touch with Cecily. It was another twenty years before she even met her son's children.

The estrangement was brought to closure in 2021 when, on Cecily's 88th birthday, she was diagnosed with cancer, which had spread to multiple locations. Cecily died four months later, in April 2021. During those final four months, her son and his family, together with Cecily's two daughters, their families, and her former husband, all came together to spend time with her. Their presence in those few months was a priceless gift for Cecily, and she made the most of it, offsetting the reality of the palliative care she received at home.

During our twenty-year interlude at Port Elliot, Cecily, a soprano, had joined a local choir and performed with them regularly. Through her choir friends, Cecily met Peter Tillett, a fine pianist, and Thomas Edmonds, a well-known tenor, from whom she had some singing lessons. Cecily was also Reiki practitioner and had joined a women's group to discuss and to explore healing in general. They became treasured friends for Cecily and they all spent quite a lot of time with her in those last months, giving her both comfort and pleasure.

Aside from many conversations with my mentor, Dr Bevan Reid MD, I had no response from well-known publishers because I had no academic credentials to support my views. One of the trainers at AIM (The Australian Institute of Management) in North Sydney, had met David Bohm during a visit to the UK and arranged for me to have a brief phone conversation with David Bohm and Basil Hiley.

In 2004 I spoke with Basil Hiley about Bohm's Implicate Order and described my Samapatti experience with the traumatised cat. I asked him how he would describe that experience in terms of physics. He said the only word in physics that could be relevant to that experience would be quantum entanglement, and that word, entanglement, encouraged me to continue my search for answers.

There have been moments in my life when someone has asked me a question and I answer it immediately, realising that I hadn't known the answer until I was asked the question. This has been my own persisting enigma of consciousness because I had thought everyone thought this way, and I am not the same, whatever that means.

As I will explain throughout this book, I was unable to explain my 'strange mind' until 1986 when I was introduced to the Yoga Sutras of Patanjali after joining a yoga class. Coincidently, I found a poster in the AIM bookshop, advertising Pandit Usharbuddh Arya's book, *Samadhi-Pada*.[3] I ordered a copy from the publisher and for me it was a new world to explore.

I had joined an evening class on the Yoga sutras, and during one of the class sessions there was a discussion about Dr Bevan Reid, a cancer researcher at the University of Sydney who claimed to have proved the presence of 'active information' in the space of his laboratory. My yoga teacher knew Dr Reid, and gave me Dr Reid's phone number, which I called. We spoke for half an hour and agreed to continue the conversation on the following weekend.

From then on, Dr Bevan Reid became my mentor, and had recommended I read David Bohm's *Wholeness and the Implicate Order*[5] because it had much in common with the science around his (Reid's) research, and was all about the thoughts that would eventually support an explanation of my experiences as a healer in the mid-1980's.

After my book, *"Thinking on the Other Side of Zero,"* was placed on the web, I contacted the publisher of the Journal of Consciousness Experiments and Research (JCER) in the USA, who invited me to join the editorial board. I contributed some essays with an emphasis on Samadhi and Samapatti on Consciousness and the Yoga Sutras to his journal, until 2019.

Much later, in the middle of 2021, my AIM colleague sent me a veritable treasure; it was an online link to the Fetzer Memorial Trust film, *"Infinite Potential: The Life & Ideas of David Bohm*[9]*."* As I watched that film, I became intrigued by Bohm's search for an explanation of Wholeness and the Implicate Order from the perspective of physics, because I was convinced his work had already demonstrated wholeness and Bohm clearly disagreed with my view.

Now, drawn by his observation *'that an explanation will come from outside of physics,'* I decided this was the time to provide my own explanation of Bohm's enigma, and to explain why Bohm had been unable to supply an explanation that would be acceptable to physicists and philosophers alike.

I have been following a similar path for most of my life, asking much the same questions and being unable to find an answer. From what I saw in the film, I thought Bohm had been in a comparable situation to me; that of being absolutely certain of something, and not knowing the source of his/my certainty.

My certainty has been about needing an explanation for how and why I think differently, and the explanation began to build itself incrementally after I read the first edition of the Yoga Sutras of Patanjali, Samadhi-pada[3], by Pandit Usharbuddh Arya, (with an introduction by Swami Rama which included a diagram of the descent of consciousness into matter). His book has since been republished after the author had reached the status of Swami and became Swami Veda Bharati. When I refer to his book throughout this one, I will refer to him as SVB.

My reason for finding the Yoga Sutras relevant to Bohm's Wholeness and the Implicate Order, comes from the purpose of Patanjali's yoga sutras themselves, which is to describe 'the descent of consciousness into matter.' I thought this statement of purpose would be enough to concern physicists and philosophers alike, because the word yoga is thought to relate to physical exercise, which is very different from consciousness, mind, memory. I assumed that for physicists and philosophers, consciousness, mind, memory are measurable correlates of neural activity in the brain and form the basis for the existing theory of mind.

In the Bohm film[9], I saw Bohm's collaboration with Hiley and physicists, with the Dalai Lama, and with Krishnamurti, as a practical way of having a sounding board upon which he might assess his ideas about wholeness, and to understand why he was so certain that wholeness was a valid concept from his perspective. I wondered why his idea had continued to remain incomplete, and as I thought about Bohm's explanation of wholeness from the perspective of my own life experience, I thought his explanation was clearly answered in SVB's Yoga book, as indeed it would be explained in almost any of the traditional Hindu philosophies for that matter.

At no point in the film did Bohm mention the Yoga sutras, and I think it more likely that Krishnamurti had assumed Bohm, had 'got it,' in view of the certainty Bohm had shown for his concept of Wholeness and the Implicate Order. The more I thought about what I saw in the film, the more I realised that the way a person develops on a path to the reach a higher state of consciousness is to control the mind by being focused on only one thing.

In yoga, concentration on just one thing is the first step into Samadhi, albeit 'Samadhi with seed,' and we can reach that state without knowing that when the mind is intensely focused it becomes a form of meditation. Any person's life experience will reflect any progress and attainment reached on that path, and it can be difficult for his peers to recognise that person has reached a seemingly unrelated goal in this other discipline.

For a physicist like Bohm, it must have been troubling to realise his own certainty, and to know there was little prospect of being able to supply an explanation that could be confirmed by the physics and/or philosophy of his peers. In my view, Bohm must have known his certainty as fact, and yet, in his own mind, he didn't understand why he was so certain that wholeness and its related natural order are valid. Nonetheless, he was certain of his position on that question, and for that reason he decided that an explanation would only come from an observer who does not think like a physicist.

Bohm's issue at hand was in the term, wholeness, and I am inviting you, the reader, to join me in considering reality from this unfamiliar perspective of wholeness in the context of the whole of everything. I had already recognised the wholeness he was talking about, not from Bohm's perspective, but from the perspective of the ancient ones who had obviously asked the same questions physicists ask today. Theirs was a perspective shared by others in that ancient community, thousands of years before our time.

This ancient perspective exists in the Yoga sutras of Patanjali[3], mentioned in the start of this Introduction, and despite being an enigma for me, I am confident that Patanjali will provide me with logical answers to these questions. The ancient ones had discovered this 'other' knowledge and had proven its validity by having others in their community replicate that 'other knowledge' as a direct experience in the Samadhi state. Patanjali tells us that anyone can learn to reach this Samadhi state and will find it to be knowledge from 'the other side of Zero' in physics, but physics, nonetheless if that is your viewpoint.

Proof from 'direct experience' is possible for someone in a Samadhi state such as Samapatti because in that state the two minds coalesce, which affords the seer and the subject the ability to 'know experientially,' that experience. If it were to be experienced subjectively by a person not in that state, it would qualify as a valid form of proof of the theory of mind and consciousness, but as the reader will see, that is not possible without being in the Samadhi state.

I know I must find a way to explain the difficulties faced in supplying a coherent understanding of Bohm's Implicate Order, and these difficulties come from the way western physicists and philosophers think about mind and consciousness. When I think about academia's definitions about spacetime, energy, mind, I am reminded of the quote from Oscar Wilde[10], 'to define is to limit,' and while he may not have had wholeness in mind, I think it can be relevant in this book. The existing Theory of mind, as a definition, is what has created what is an incomplete theory.

The Hard Problem of Consciousness[11] is a thorny issue for philosophers and will remain so until academia can think from a new perspective, which might allow them to imagine or hypothesise an answer from outside of physics (and philosophy) and to learn to think in the way the ancient ones thought. That is what I will do with this book, and I make no promises about avoiding stepping on anyone's toes.

Years ago, I watched a video of Krishnamurti and Bohm discussing the state of the world, and both agreed that the way the world is at any point in time will always be the direct result of the way we think. They concluded that to achieve any valid form of change for the better, we must think without limits of any kind. I can still remember having conversations with friends in which the listener would interject with, "but Alan, you can't say that!"

Now the questions have evolved, creating even more questions:

'Where do I find this entirely unique way?'

'How does one think in that unique way?'

'What does thinking uniquely mean?"

Unique from whose perspective?'

It just goes on and on. I agree that wholeness must include every way of thinking, and I accept that these questions will be difficult for readers too. The same can be said of Bohm's wholeness, when he had already concluded that any valid answer would come from 'outside of physics.'

The ancient ones had already thought in terms of the cosmos, physics, mind, memory, and consciousness, not to mention identity, self, self-interest, others, relationships, spacetime, space, astronomy, black holes, mind, memory, consciousness, quantum mechanics, philosophy, medicine, chemistry, order, and wholeness.

I could ask the physicists and philosophers, 'what if Bohm is right about wholeness? What then?' Surely wholeness must include you, me, everyone, everything, nothing, everywhere, nowhere, infinity, classical physics, and quantum physics.

Can you see what Bohm was getting at? Wholeness.

It is not a question of asking whether wholeness is outside of physics; it might simply be that the way physicists think about physics is from a viewpoint which is, by definition, outside of wholeness. This is not an unthinkable concept; it is simply another way of looking at reality without any of the conventional constraints and boundaries we have created.

This book is not about the yoga sutras of Patanjali as their teachers explain them; I am writing about a fundamental process that is inseparable from wholeness, which I believe can help us understand what Bohm knew intuitively and how and why he knew it. Bohm and Hiley had likened wholeness to a hologram. Patanjali's Yoga sutras have been the missing piece of the hologram puzzle in my own personal quest to understand why and how I think differently.

I expect that by explaining my own understanding of reality, based on the translation of Sankhya[4] given by GS, and a secondary school education with a smattering of the quantum mechanics available in the books I read, I will be able to shed some light on how and why Bohm's concept of wholeness was thinkable for him. When something is thinkable, it doesn't necessarily mean it will automatically be explainable or unexplainable, but if we seek an answer from the perspective of Patanjali, we will find the right question to supply its right answer (or vice versa).

In terms of pages written, the book is not very long, but I give fair warning that it will challenge its reader to form an understanding of the way she or he thinks, and I expect it will be useful in that respect. This is my reason for placing this objective challenge in this Introduction.

In that same degree of fairness, I make no claims or disclaimers about what I have written, other than to say it is about my life, lived in ignorance of how, and why, I am who I am. From the perspective of wholeness, I intent no disrespect. I respect all beliefs, all faiths, and all Gods. A belief in one God, Brahma, Yahweh, Allah, etc., and that belief is universal, and as such, one's respect for a name is universal and personal.

I leave any response to what I have written to you, the reader, and I do not expect anyone to live by any of the rules you may assume me to have. That said, as humans, we are all individually responsible for our own mind, and our responses, conscious and unconscious. So, sit here, comfortably outside of physics, and read at your own unconditional pace.

CHAPTER 1

An introduction to my difference

This chapter is twofold: first to introduce me as one whose life experiences are ordinary in some respects and extraordinary in others. From the perspective of the people who, for reasons only they could explain, asked me for the kind of help not readily available to them, they were extraordinary. In other respects, what I have learned from the Yoga sutras of Patanjali[3] applies to those experiences as an accidental healer, and fortuitously, to the issue of Wholeness and an Implicate Order[5] raised by David Bohm. At first, all individual experiences are unrelated to other individuals, and yet, in the spirit of Bohm's Wholeness everything is related.

I will begin with my early childhood because I don't remember any of it before the age of four or five. What I do remember is my being brought to a kindergarten held in a church hall in Williamstown, Victoria, Australia. All I remember about that is that it was a happy place with friendly children. I must have been five at that time, which was at the end of 1939. The following year I started as St Mary's Catholic School in the infants class and I must have skipped a grade at some point because when my family left Williamstown in September or October in 1945 I was in grade 5.

We moved to Mount Erica in Gippsland where my father had taken a job at Sharp's sawmill to operate the steam engine powering the sawmill, and another steam powered winch which dragged logs from the mountainside. The sawmill was at least twenty-five miles from the small town of Erica, only connected to the town by a narrow-gauge line operated by the State Forestry, with no access to a school.

My brother Jim and I played in the bush and on a huge hill of sawdust dispersed from the mill. When that sawmill closed six months later we moved to a house two miles from the town of Erica. We started at the State School in Erica in1946; the school had just two rooms and I was placed in grade 5 again because we had not attended any school while living on the mountain.

The one consistent feeling I have had since then was my certainty that the way I think was always out of step with the members of my family, and with everyone else I knew. I had grown up accepting my family's opinion that my mind was a bit 'defective,' and they, my neighbours and schoolmates, all treated me as if it were true. I have accepted it all my life, and from thinking that way, I become whatever others believed me to be. In retrospect, I can see that people have always got the Alan who acted according to their assessments and expectations of him, and for a long time I didn't know that was happening.

This changed in my early 60s when Cecily and I had moved to Queensland to live on a 40-acre block and we set up a hobby farm. My eldest brother, Gordon had come to help us put up a shed, and one evening the issue of how I think came up in a conversation with my wife Cecily and Gordon, when Cecily asked him,

'Gordon, has Alan always been different in the way he thinks?'

'Yes, he's always been that way.' he replied. 'Ever since his convulsions.'

2

I jumped in then. 'When did I have convulsions? I didn't know that happened to me too.'

'What do you mean, to me too?' Cecily asked both of us.

I replied, 'All I ever knew was that we had two brothers, Billy and Peter, who died from convulsions before I was born, that was during the Great Depression, and a lot of kids suffered from that condition at the time.'

Gordon cut in,

'How would you know? You were only about four then. You went to hospital just as sick as them, and we had written you off because we didn't expect you to live either. When you came home from hospital you were a different kid. You didn't understand anything we said. It was as if your mind was empty; you didn't know the things you knew before you went to hospital. We had to draw pictures of things before you could understand an idea or anything else.'

Cecily nodded,

'That would explain a lot of things Alan, but it doesn't mean the way you think is defective. It may even be quite the opposite.'

'Ha, if only.' I said with a wry smile.

Years later, I asked my mentor, Dr Bevan Reid MD, about febrile convulsions and he agreed that during the Great Depression, children having febrile-convulsions was common, and the convulsions related to the child having an extremely elevated temperature, and in my case, there was the potential for dire consequences for the developing brain of this four-year-old Alan.

Obviously, I didn't die, but it is possible that in my case, the 'dire consequence' was a near-death experience; I think that would account for my inability to know and remember the things I had known before the convulsions. It is an interesting thought, but how to define what I had lost, or how to imagine a way to measure it then, would have been difficult or impossible.

My mind is always empty and only becomes engaged by the presence of any immediate momentary input, as if it has little awareness of me; from my perspective it has always been that way. There were no MRI scanners then and X-rays were rare around that time. I looked up the hospital on the web to check if there were records of children with convulsions during that period; sadly, it was demolished years ago, along with all of its patient records.

Recently, I had an acupuncture treatment and during his examination of my tongue the practitioner commented on its deep cracks/fissures, saying that, according to traditional Oriental medicine, these cracks are consistent with having a sustained elevated temperature as a young child.

If I did have a Near Death experience, as Gordon's description suggests, then it would seem that my neural network would have been compromised, as indicated by the fact that I didn't know anything from my life experience prior to the convulsions. Moreover, this also resonates with my mostly 'empty mind.' That 'normally' empty mind would also account for my being 'established' in the Samadhi state, as 'one who is born that way' (in Samadhi), rather than one attaining Samadhi through meditation and study with an accredited guru.

Now, coming back to the issue of how I think, the Fetzer film mentioned in chapter 1 brought this issue to mind, and from what I had seen in that film, I had assumed that Bohm had been intuitively aware that the way to explain his Implicate Order must already exist in an ordered reality.

I base my assumption of Bohm's intuitive awareness on my own research, which had led to me read the yoga sutras of Patanjali[1] in which the author/commentator says, *that every aspect of what was known in the past, is currently known, and what will become known in the future, already exists, and can be known at any time by anyone in the Samadhi state.'*

In the film, Bohm had mentioned that any explanation of the Implicate Order would come from outside of physics, and I think most would agree that the Yoga Sutras of Patanjali[3] are, superficially at least, outside of physics. Bohm also suggested that the Implicate Order is part of a process, and I can understand why he thought that process would work within a greater whole.

In my own mind, I think he had hoped to find an explanation for his belief in wholeness as a fundamental of reality itself, and in his need to be able to explain it, even to himself.

Thus, my reasons for drafting this book are:

a. to justify my assumption about Bohm's intuitive awareness by clarifying what that assumption teaches me about the way I think rather than inferring something about Bohm

b. to explain wholeness through what I have learned from Patanjali's Yoga sutras, in terms of Bohm's theoretically whole reality

c. to present what I have come to know from my experiences in the Samadhi state, and why they show that I do think differently to the people I know

d. to show how all of this supports Bohm's concept of an Implicate Order as a fundamental part of a whole reality

e. and to show what is the process alluded to by Bohm

f. and to have you, the reader, share in what I find along this journey.

I will write what I have learned over the years, not necessarily in the order listed in the reasons given above, but to keep in mind my premise that Bohm's Implicate Order must, logically, be inseparable from the philosophies used in Patanjali's Yoga sutras and Sankhya, and in the Vedas, Buddhism, Torah, Bible and Koran for that matter, because of its wholeness. I believe it can remain compared to physics if one is prepared to recognise that the spiritual narrative of the Yoga sutras is actually describing interactions between actual moments in quantum information within the unmanifested energy, and I can only do that incrementally, not as a complete introduction.

From my perspective, wholeness is a composite of a fundamental process, that not only creates experiences as well as matter and forces within spacetime, but it is simultaneously the (infolding and unfolding) of all experiences, matter and forces, past, present and future, as a nonlocal potential for all of that. From that perspective we need to get used to becoming familiar with words like 'everything' and 'nothing' in terms of infinity, at least mentally familiar with them if we are ever going to think in this 'unusual way.'

I am not an academic, but I can understand Bohm's Implicate Order as it relates to wholeness, consciousness, mind, and memory. I am reminded of Oscar Wilde's quote, 'to define is to limit,' and I can't logically accept that an understanding of wholeness 'within limits' would be what Bohm wanted.

Instead, I will examine wholeness from a perspective 'without limits,' as far as western understanding is concerned, and while I know he said such understanding would be outside of physics, it is not out of physics at all if one can accept that wholeness includes what I had previously called 'the other side of zero' (in the absence of a non-academic perspective).

Put simply, it means there can be other ways to interpret things we cannot fully understand, within the 'limits' imposed on us by our western interpretation of physics and philosophy. I think of the old adage which went something like, 'to use something as a lever or method over time, will have you the user, becoming that lever or method.' Technology changes over time but we still become the 'process.'

Just take computers, TV, phone apps and social media as examples; where would we be without any of them? Their inherent danger is that their accessibility has made them become a common language, which has morphed incrementally into a common system of belief, where truth is measured by the ratio of the number of likes to dislike.

My 'way' to understand Bohm's questions appeared as I tried to understand them in terms of my experiences as an accidental healer, and my understanding grew of itself from having to learn by doing, rather than having a teacher show me what to do. I do not expect you, the reader, to replicate my experiences because that would involve entering the same Samadhi state and one cannot learn that from reading a book.

What may make this explanation of parts of the Yoga sutras difficult for the reader is the terminology used, and I will address this as we go, beginning with the opening words of the Sutra from SVB's commentary, which is explaining memory to a student of the Yoga sutras.

The reader must know that the way the Yoga sutras are taught in an ashram is through a combination of spoken words and mind to mind communication between the teacher and the student. To be accepted as a student, the student will have completed a thorough study of the Vedas and other spiritual texts, and to be assessed as competent.

The first Sutra begins with the Sanskrit word, *atha*, which means now. This is a significant word because it indicates a beginning and also means a transition to a new level of understanding. My intention is to introduce the possibility of that kind of transition in the way we think.

My position in all my earlier writing was to suggest my experiences in Samapatti imply that the accepted view about consciousness is incomplete, and to further suggest we might address that incompleteness through considering experiences which don't fit that current model. In my view, any theory of consciousness must include the questions of:

1. Does consciousness enter the mind through processes within the brain?
2. Why do we regard consciousness as a subjective state?
3. Could consciousness be part of a fundamental feature of reality itself?

To answer these questions, I will move on to chapter 2 and begin by providing some of my experiences in Samapatti which clearly are outside of the existing theory of mind and consciousness.

CHAPTER 2

An accidental healer

In the early 1980's I attended a series of seminars called Est., and, like all the other participants, I was seeking something different. My life had been turned upside down after my divorce from a marriage of 22 years, I was in debt, and I faced the prospect of bankruptcy. I thought it was my chance to clean the slate, and I began this next phase by throwing out everything I had kept for more than three months from my former life, hoping work and the seminars would supply the rest.

That hoping worked for a week until a work colleague asked me to come to lunch at his home on the weekend; he explained his wife had been hit by a car driven by a drunk, and had been hospitalised with brain injuries, part amputation of one leg, and other internal injuries. He said he had noticed I was always calm and competent when I serviced his typesetting system and wondered if I could help his wife.

I agreed to come, not from any sense I might be able to help but because he seemed so desperate; I was just a parent at a loose end with an empty slate and no plans. I arrived at his home and was led into the kitchen to sit beside his wife Joy, who was huddled in a wheelchair and visibly traumatised. She had been in hospital for around a month, recovering from the injuries and this was his first opportunity to bring her home for a weekend of respite.

As I sat beside Joy, John began a conversation, saying the medical opinion was that Joy was becoming a 'vegetable,' but as his conversation continued, I thought it might be that she was a difficult patient trying to adjust to a difficult change in her life without any help from her husband, who could only think about fixing her unfixable body and mind. As John continued talking it became obvious he wanted to tell me how the insurance claim would relieve Joy's discomfort if and when she was able to leave the hospital.

"They have not been able to do much for her in a month, and I would rather have her here at home. There's not much they can do for her brain damage and with her physical damage she will always need the wheelchair." he said.

I thought, what he really knows is that Joy is incapacitated to quite an extent with her brain injuries, and that she is a difficult patient in a hospital ward not equipped to deal with her needs.

As he talked, Joy looked at me and shrugged.

"The way it is, is the way it is."

I thought, she is not a vegetable; from where I am sitting, I see a woman who knows exactly the extent of her injuries and the effects of those injuries. I can see she is frustrated by the fact that the hospital staff are not equipped to manage her in a hospital ward environment and she wants desperately to be cared for at home.

Her husband doesn't understand because she is still unable to speak clearly due to her unresolved head injuries and the pain of her trauma. I could see that both her hands were tightly clenched with the fingernails cutting into her palms, and I realised that part of Joy is still in the moment of her accident.

For me, this was quite a lesson about the conceptual difference between mind and body, and that her mind is more capable than John knows.

He can only see her physical state reflecting her injuries, and his assumptions about them. I stayed with them for the rest of the day and went home later that night.

Thinking about this visit later, I remembered that the focus of John's conversation had been around getting carers and waiting for the insurance claim to be finalised and paid out. Initially, John had been given some help from one of their neighbours caring for Joy for two weeks and that worked for Joy because she had a close friendship with that lady. But the caring neighbour's family needed her too and she had to stop caring for Joy after two weeks. John's next step was to engage professional carers but Joy was never satisfied with the new carers. What John had missed was the fact that Joy also had to cope with her change of circumstance, as well as his own change of circumstance. As for Joy's perspective, that didn't exist.

A month later on one of my visits I asked,

"Joy, why do you think you had this accident?"

"So that John could stay home and look after me."

She said that so matter-of-factly and John was obviously surprised.

I looked at him and asked,

"What do you think about that John"?

"I can't do that; I have to work and pay the bills."

"Is there another way John?"

"None that I can see," he said.

I thought about that and asked him,

"Have you spoken to your bank manager?"

"No, what could he do anyway?"

"You could get a loan on the house, supported by the impending resolution of the insurance claim. He might even be able to chase that up for you."

To his credit, John did see the bank manager, and was able to secure a bank loan, and leave his job to become Joy's full-time home-care provider. I visited him and his wife and two children as often as I could, more as company and someone for them to talk to.

oOo

In 1984 a new healing situation arose after a friend from the Est seminars, Emma, wanted to talk with me, explaining she had discovered a breast lump, which was later diagnosed as breast cancer. Like John, she thought I was calm, and assumed I could make her calm too. We arranged to meet on weekends for coffee and a chat; the main issue for Emma was having to decide whether to have chemotherapy, and underneath that was the inevitable fear of death.

By now, without any training in counselling I had accepted this informal role of counsellor, and was becoming confident that answers would come if I didn't try to find them; I knew I had to find how to give Emma a way to make her own decision, and what worked for me was letting the words come without thinking and doing or saying whatever I said or did at the time. She had come to expect these mind-stretching conversations, referring to them as our Creative Dying Workshop.

During one of those conversations about helping Emma to decide what to do about chemotherapy I heard myself saying,

"Emma, imagine you are a tree beside a road and a car has crashed into you. How do you, the tree, cope with what is a significant injury?"

She replied,

"I would ask myself to share the trauma across the whole of my trunk and limbs, that way each part of me would have a chance to manage the pain in every part of me as a small local pain."

Then she 'freaked out' as she responded with the tree's answer.

"That was a sneaky one Alan!"

"Without knowing what I was doing, I have decided to have chemotherapy; what is even scarier, I have never thought like that before. How did you do it?"

"Well Emma, for what it's worth, I don't think I've ever thought that way before either, so I don't know how I did it."

In the following month, Emma accepted her decision, had the chemotherapy sessions, and we continued our coffee sessions for the duration of her chemotherapy. Happily, after about six months the lump in her breast had subsided and she resumed her acting roles and was able to take whatever casual office work was available at the time.

Our coffee sessions continued, and eventually she became more relaxed. We talked about this change and her opinion was that I had somehow taken her into an altered state; I had thoughts along the same lines, but there were so many questions that I really needed a starting point, and I had no idea what that point might be. Every chat had a surprise and I could only keep doing it because somehow or other, every question inferred an answer coming from a common source and I wondered if I had been looking in the wrong place; can it be that this is not Emma's problem at all, am I the problem? I just didn't know.

The next time I visited Emma it was at her home, and we talked about what she had called her altered state. I asked her to close her eyes and go back to that state, whatever it was. Emma became relaxed and I asked her, "When was the first time you saw your mother?"

I was surprised to hear myself ask that question and had no idea what made me ask it at all. It clearly had surprised Emma, because she immediately sat up with her eyes open, and in almost total disbelief, she said,

"Alan, I just saw the smile on my mother's face in what must have been in the moments after I was born. It was when the midwife showed me to her. What is even more surprising for me was to see the love for me on my mother's face, a love I have always doubted ever existed."

I was taken by surprise too; I had not thought to ask about the first time she had seen her mother. I had only thought to ask Emma about her relationship with her mother, and instead I heard myself ask this question about their relationship. I didn't ask when, or what happened at a specific time, so that rules out any suggestion on my part. For Emma, her answer was her description of what was really a revelation, one which had completely altered her belief about her mother.

For all the time I had known her, Emma held the belief that she had never seen her mother smile at her, and over time had become convinced that her mother had never loved her and now that belief was gone. As the cancer progressed this altered state became our normal practice to lessen her pain; Emma called it 'zapping out' because she thought she was out of her body and free from its pain.

It did not free me from anything though; I was as much in the dark as Emma was so far as explaining this 'altered state' was concerned, and I will talk more about Emma later on because she taught me so much through the questions arising from each visit.

In September 1985, I had a casual job with IBM, doing odd jobs in the location department of IBM's North Sydney office. As a casual job, it was for only one year and had come to its end. It had been a simple role that gave me plenty of time to think, and I was looking forward to a change. I went to a job centre to see what was available and saw a notice advertising a 10-day Vipassana meditation course in the Blue Mountains. It was residential, and it was free!

I phoned the number, enrolled, and did the course which involved sitting silently on a wooden floor in a cold classroom to meditate all day, breaking only for meals. There was no talking, not even at mealtime or in the sleeping rooms. To be honest, sitting on the floor was physically painful, but the lecture given by the teacher at the end of each day was far more lucid than those at est, and the Buddhism he taught made sense to me.

A week later, I met a couple of women who had set up a healing centre in their house, and I went there daily and we talked about healing. One of them (Hanta) had a recurring headache that presented every time it was raining. I sat with her on one of those days and asked,

"When was the first time you had this headache Hanta?"

"I was living in South Africa at the time and had arranged to go to a dance with a boyfriend. Before he came to take me, someone else offered to drive me to the dance because of the rain, and I accepted his offer. On the way to the dance we had a car accident in which I had bumped my head on the dashboard."

"I never saw the boyfriend again because I was too embarrassed."

"Well Hanta, perhaps your mind relates the headache, the rain, your embarrassment and the bump on your head, to the fact that you broke your agreement to go to the dance with your boyfriend."

"If you can accept that truth, the headache can go away."

I didn't realise it at the time, but the connection of the aspects of her experience reminds me of how any single one of the various aspects of an event come together as the trigger for the memory of the whole event. I can understand the context of any memory is part of the composite information related to that event.

It was through these two women that I heard about a 'psychic healing course,' starting in January of 1986. It turned out to be a class about the Yoga Sutras and was taught by James McGarry in his Hypnosis practice in Sydney's eastern suburbs. The classes were focussed on a book by I. K. Taimni, *The Science of Yoga*[12], published by the Theosophical Society.

I had a conversation with Dr Bevan Reid, Md., a cancer researcher at the University of Sydney, who became a mentor to me, following an earlier phone conversation about his cancer experiments which he had used to explore his concept of information in space.

At the time I had a started in a day job at the Australian Institute of Management in North Sydney, setting up classrooms for the trainers and attendees, and doing any other odd jobs required in the classrooms and in the Institute's bookshop. One day I came across a supplier's poster in the Institute bookshop, advertising a different book on the Yoga sutras, *"The Yoga sutras of Patanjali, Samadhi pada*[1], by Pandit Usharbuddh Arya. I ordered the book from its USA publisher, and it arrived a month later.

I found the book more interesting than Taimni's, written by an obviously accomplished teacher involved in a real yoga institute. I began reading it in my spare time and there, in its Introduction, was the yoga diagram which explained diagrammatically the creation of mind and matter in terms of spirituality, and over time it became fundamental in developing my understanding of the Yoga sutras.

My discussions with Dr Reid were productive and I could relate a lot of what he said to the subjects covered in the yoga classes, as well as to Dr Reid's work and his concept of information in space. He recommended I should read David Bohm's book, *"Wholeness and the Implicate Order,*[3]*"* which I thought had much in common with the Yoga sutras of Patanjali; I don't know why I thought that other than it seemed to be self-evident at the time.

What I didn't know was that during my Yoga classes McGarry had recognised I was already in the Samadhi state described in the Yoga books, and he could see I was 'established' in that state. During one of his lessons on that specific Yoga Sutra, YS.1.41., he had explained this state to the class and how there were two ways of entering Samapatti; the first is conventional pathway involving studying with an accredited teacher and almost continuous meditation; the second way is to have been 'born that way.'

I knew I didn't fall into the category of first way; I had no awareness of anything like that. The second way sounded like it would only apply to students in India, and logically it wouldn't apply to me anyway because I was just an ordinary but confused 52-year-old man born in Australia. He also warned the class to be aware of the distinct possibility that whatever the feelings they experienced in that state might be, while in the presence of a person who was the subject of their focus, the feeling might be interpreted as being in love with that person; it did not mean or confirm that this is what the feelings really meant.

During a class at the beginning of the following year, James suggested I could help a fellow student who had asked him if he knew what might be done for her traumatised cat. This event remains a surprising one for me; on the one hand it has led to my experiences in that Samapatti state as described by Patanjali, while on the other hand I thought it was a brutal way of setting up this ignorant student (me) for a very confronting lesson.

It became a journey of discovering myself using abilities I did not know I had, and I would never know I had them until they were needed in a particular circumstance, the existence of which I could not predict; the word praxis now comes to mind as I write this.

In retrospect, it seems as if the circumstance or the context itself was the teacher of aspects of a system or process which helped me learn, simply by validating Patanjali's Yoga sutras through participation. At the time, I did not have the wit needed to associate this experience with the earlier conversations I had between Emma Gray and me.

The first lesson for me was that I was not the healer. The second lesson was that I did not know what the outcome would be. The third lesson was that the system or process itself is fundamental in the absolute sense of that word, and it is what Bohm was leading toward with his Implicate Order.

What follows is a narrative of these experiences as my explanation of the retrospective paragraph above. Even the word, narrative has its own special place when we look deeper into how memory works, but for now I will let the experiences create their own questions to challenge the conventional philosophies and physics.

oOo

A disturbed cat

At this point you, the reader, needs to understand that I had taken my teacher James McGarry at his word; he had assured this woman I would be able to help her cat. I had no idea of what would happen, how I would help this cat I had never seen before, and obviously, it had never seen me before either. Even if I could help it, how and what do I do? How might the cat respond? So many what-ifs.

I took her address and agreed on a time on the following weekend, and duly arrived at her suburban flat. I followed her into a sitting room which had a chair beside a coffee table and a bean bag cushion on the floor. Motioning me to the bean bag she explained that this cat, Zac, had been with her for a little over a year and was obviously suffering from a life of trauma and abuse. She explained it would not sit on her lap for more than a minute, it did not miaow, it snarled, and in all that year the cat had never washed itself.

As I settled into the bean bag she returned with this very shabby smelly cat and placed it on my lap. I looked at the grey tabby cat and without thinking I placed my hand on its head. To my surprise, the cat immediately went to sleep, and at once I began to experience flashing lights in my head. This was a surprise for me; I have never had mental images of anything at any time in my life and I wondered, how does this work?

The flashing lights remained for about twenty minutes, eventually giving way to an unreal garden scene. The grass/plants were larger than normal, and where I would have expected green plants there was a normal garden area in shades of yellow, brown and red. I realised I was seeing the garden from the cat's eye-level and colour perspective and it immediately changed to my perspective with normal colours and physical dimensions.

I knew I had never seen this garden before, and at the same time I knew the garden was a familiar, safe, and comfortable place. After about twenty minutes in the cat's mental garden, I knew the cat would wake up. I opened my eyes and watched as it woke up, stretched its back and legs and began to wash itself.

There was a combination of astonishment and relief on its owners face; I have no idea what my face looked like, I just wanted to get out of there before she asked how it happened. I accepted her offer of coffee and sipped the coffee rather than talk during those uncomfortable minutes of mock detachment.

At the next Yoga class, time was taken up by her description of how her cat was before and is now. I referred their questions to me back to James, but my classmates had already decided I was a healer. James just played it cool; this was exactly what he had taught us about Samapatti.

oOo

Tachycardia

My next experience was a more moderate event. My flatmate Susan was having a tachycardia episode, explaining that she had them occasionally and asked if I could help. I did not know how I could help, I just sat down beside her on the floor, placing one of my hands over her heart and the other on her back behind her heart and waited to see what would happen. I was aware of her fast heartbeat and thought about my own slower heart rate.

My hands got quite hot for a while and then, as they cooled down her heart slowed to what I guessed was a normal heart rate. I was aware of a keen sense of love during the whole time, and this surprised me because I knew I wasn't in love with her. I realised it was the side effect of the focus James had warned about in his Yoga classes; for me it was another lesson.

oOo

A knitting of bone

Soon after the tachycardia episode I was contacted by an Est., friend who asked if I might be able to help one of her friends. She explained her friend had a fracture of the tibia which had failed to knit after the insertion of a steel pin at the fracture site which was inserted to aid the bone to knit. She had given me the phone number to call, and I phoned her friend and arranged a meeting to see if I could help her.

I went to her flat and she explained an appointment had been made to X-ray the fracture in a week's time to see if there had been any change, and if there was no change, other options would need to be considered. She had hoped I might be able to help the bone to knit and asked what I would do. I told her I didn't know what I could do, saying it is always a matter of seeing what happens and I have no method other than letting whatever happens, happen.

I sat down facing her and looked at her leg, then I closed my eyes and asked her to close her eyes. I had a sense the fracture was in a state of trauma; it was a memory of the trauma which had caused the fracture. With my eyes closed, I thought about that part of her leg and knew it had a dark kind of pain. Then I thought the darkness might dissipate if I covered it with some bright sunny light. Then I knew I should open my eyes and was confronted with this extremely excited woman, who told me that she had watched me replace this dark 'energy' with bright yellow 'energy.' I wondered how my thought of darkness had become bright yellow energy in her mind, which she had mentally watched happen in her leg.

Reflecting on this event I can say that from her description of what she 'saw' me do; she had seen visually what I had only thought. At the time, I didn't know what she had visualised, and I didn't see what I was thinking because I have never been able to visualise anything. I couldn't explain how these two unrelated events manifested separately as a composite simultaneous event. The following week she called me after her X-ray to tell me there was evidence of knitting at the fracture site. We will never know if it was something I had done, or if it was the natural result of the bone knitting at the fracture site.

oOo

Huntington's chorea

Anne Bailey, a psyche nurse who was one of my colleagues from the Yoga class, had a patient with Huntington's chorea and asked me to see if I could help him. We arranged a place where I could meet Anne's patient Graham, and as usual, I explained to him I did not know how this works, but if we are patient we can find out if he can be helped. His partner made us coffee and we sat down to see if I might be able to have an influence on his shaking.

I focused my attention on Graham, and initially I started to shake like Graham was shaking. I realised it was Graham's shaking and my shaking stopped. Using trial and error, I found that by sitting across the room two of three metres from him, and just being focused on him, his shaking did reduce enough to be noticed, and this became our practice. Little by little, we found his shaking would stop for periods of up to 45 minutes with me keeping my focus on him; we did this once a week for a month.

I suggested he should focus on his experience of the shaking stopping, to embed it as a memory; my hope being that by recalling this absence of shaking, he could use it to give a result like the one he had from the session. It did help and he was able to 'practice' the session at home by remembering the periods of no shaking.

Over time he had made sufficient demonstrable progress through remembering the session, and his doctor gave him leave to move from the live-in clinic to his partner's house. With more sessions and home practice he developed enough confidence to accept the offer of a clerical job and earn an income. Later, he and his partner decided to take a holiday and promised to keep doing the memory sessions daily. They asked me what I would do next after they had left for their holiday. I heard myself saying,

"I won't be doing this anymore; I want to know how it all works. I'm not a healer; I can't teach anyone if I don't know how it all works."

Having said that, I realised I had heard what I had said before I knew what I was going to say; I had started to find the answer to my question before I knew I even had a question. As I thought about that conundrum, I realised that the answer and the question must always exist together, part of the same process and separated only by how the question is framed and asked, and I thought this might be related to how the mind works. By this time, I had realised that my mind is empty, or, if not empty, then at least it is not consciously active. I had starting to keep notes of my thoughts and over time writing became my own instrument of exploration and learning.

I found an online journal which was on the same path and sent essays which were published. That continued for almost ten years, bringing me into contact with other contributors. Those I found most helpful were originally from India; Dr Syamala Hari, who had worked at Bell Laboratories in the USA, and Meera Chakravorty, a Sanskrit scholar in India. Both had read my descriptions of my experiences, and both agreed I was 'established' in the Samadhi state of Samapatti during those experiences, and that I was in the category of 'having been born that way.'

oOo

Recreational magic

The next experience came from a casual conversation with Est friends, Pauline and Henry, while we were having dinner one evening. It was Pauline who asked me,

"Alan, tell us some of the magical stories about you healing people?

I said, "Magic is something we can only demonstrate through experiences, not just by words Pauline, so forget about healing because that requires someone having pain."

"O.K. Alan, how can you demonstrate your magic?"

"I'm not magic, but if you want a demonstration of what I have done we can all do that tonight after we get home. All we have do is to agree to meet somewhere in a dream tonight, and Pauline, you can choose a place to for us meet, but don't tell us where that is because we need to find that out in our dreams."

"We can agree on a time to meet, let us say midnight tonight, and next time we meet we can compare our experiences to see if any of it has worked."

Pauline and Henry agreed. I drove home and didn't get to bed until after midnight, and in my dream, I saw the meeting place, somewhere I knew I had never seen before, and I knew they had realised I was late.

The following week we met to compare notes, and I gave Pauline and Henry my description of the meeting place; Pauline and Henry described meeting at the same place and both knew I had arrived late.

oOo

I continued seeing Emma more often after the cancer had resurfaced; she had become unable to work or act in plays, although she had made herself available to the university medical school as a cancer patient. This supplied a part of her life which she felt should help others in a comparable situation.

It was through Emma volunteering as a cancer patient at the medical school that resulted in two palliative care nurses being asked to visit Emma at home. The outcome of that visit led to her admission to a palliative care facility just a week later. Soon

after her admission Emma called me to ask me to visit so I could 'Zap her out,' which was her phrase for going into her 'altered state.' (In my day job I worked an afternoon shift at AIM, finishing usually between 9 and 10pm, which allowed me time to go to Emma's hospice after work).

Arriving there, I found an extremely nervous Emma in a single room, propped up in bed with tubes in her nose, and her eyes fixed on the gauge of the oxygen bottle set up beside her bed. I sat with her throughout the night and she was able to finally relax and go to sleep.

I visited her every night over a period of about three months, and with patience and zapping her out, Emma got more relaxed from the morphine and from accepting her situation in the hospice. Oftentimes, Emma just settled down in her bed and we talked until I 'zapped her out; then she went to sleep. I remembered our early conversations about cancer when she talked about having no confidence in faith, and what she really wanted in her situation was certainty.

We had talked about how to reach that certainty, and at the time I had said we needed to make that our starting point rather than the destination. It was one of those unthought statements without an explanation, and only now I realise that I could see even then that certainty was beginning to manifest itself for Emma.

She had one of her actor friends bring Shakespeare's plays to read, and as I walked into her room she said,

"You know Alan, that Richard is nasty piece of work."

"Richard who, Emma?" I asked.

"Richard the Third," she said seriously.

I remembered that for the first three weeks in hospital she had refused all visitors other than her acting friends. Having some measure of control over who visited her had given Emma a sense of security. This was strengthened by what she saw in the level of commitment the staff applied in their caring for her. This had the effect of cutting the stress that coping by herself had generated for her during and after her chemotherapy. If all it took to heal cancer was this exceptional level of caring by the nurses, their patients would have been able to dance out of the hospital in a week; unfortunately, this was not the case.

Eventually the staff asked me to persuade others to visit and spend time with her because she had come to want someone with her all the time. I asked Emma who I should ask and she agreed to have me call her acting friends.

"Emma, who else should I call?"

Her reply was immediate.

"Call the Ghostbusters, Alan," she said, with a twinkle in her eyes.

Soon the days had become more difficult for her, particularly in finding a comfortable position to breathe. Now, relaxing was out of the question for Emma, and one night as I walked into her room I had started to ask if she wanted me to zap her out for a break, but she cut me off with this profound statement:

"Not a word Alan, I have an announcement to make;"

"I'm going to get married."

"Who are you going to marry Emma?"

"I'm going to marry Emma," she declared strongly.

She repeated it again the following night, and despite the pain she had come to this assertion of Self. I zapped her out and she was still sleeping when I left the following morning. As I left the hospital for what became the last time, I knew that faith had indeed given way to the certainty she had so desperately wanted.

The following evening I was at work and a nurse from the hospice called to tell me that Emma had just slipped away. I had a sense she was saying True Friend. In a minute or two, these words came to me as a poem.

> "A thief in the night?
> Never!
> Death is the gentlest of friends,
> Easing the pain,
> As only can one who truly knows me'
> for whom I really am."

A week later I attended Emma's memorial service, followed by afternoon tea, all which she had organised for herself. All her fellow actors were there, along with her Est seminar friends and two of her hospital nurses. I was surprised when the nurses pressed me to tell them about my 'relationship with Emma.'

"Alan, what is it that you were really doing with Emma every night?"

"I was just sitting with her because that is all she wanted me to do."

"No Alan, there was much more to it than just sitting with her; we watch people die all the time in our work, and we have never seen such a beautiful death."

"Alright. I know I had a beneficial effect on Emma, but I honestly do not know what it is or how it happens; there was no relationship in a physical sense, not even an emotional one. It came about when she asked if I could help her decide whether to have chemotherapy and continued from there. What we found was that Emma entered some sort of altered state. I have no idea how or why she did it; I don't know if I can say I did it because I was not conscious of doing anything in those times. I just sat and looked at her."

I was left wondering if it might be me who entered that altered state, and for some reason she was included.

Fortunately for me, the nurses did not talk to anyone else at the afternoon tea, which meant I did not have to explain myself to anyone else that afternoon. Nonetheless, I realised I would have to find the underlying cause of it soon or I would go mad. I didn't go mad, quite the opposite.

Six months after Emma died, two of my Est friends, Michael and Judy Hollingworth, invited me to their home to have dinner with them. They told me they had a Reiki healer friend they wanted me to meet.

That healer was Cecily, who I mentioned in the Introduction, and from that meeting Cecily and I became friends, and we were married in the following year, with Michael as our "Best man," and Judy as our "Best woman." That was 29 years ago.

I stayed at my job at AIM in North Sydney and Cecily continued with her Reiki practise. We moved to Queensland late in 1993 to a forty-acre block of land in the hinterland and were joined by Cecily's sister Lesley in the following year. Lesley's son, Jonathon, and his mate Richard, built our house on the block.

We needed to sell up and leave five years later after I had a double bypass operation. Lesley bought a house in the nearby town of

Montville, while Cecily and I moved to South Australia on Australia Day in 1998. Cecily hoped to be nearer to her children and we bought a 100-year-old stone house in Port Elliot.

Two years later I was still wrestling with the Yoga sutras and writing occasionally, but my focus shifted one Saturday morning when my daughter Kelly phoned to tell me my eldest daughter, Tracey, was in a coma in the Taree hospital, in New South Wales. Her body had rejected the heart and lungs transplant she had received five years earlier and her vital organs were failing. I was shaken because I had spoken to her on her birthday just two weeks earlier, and at the time she was bright and cheerful on the phone, so Kelly's call was completely unexpected.

I was able to get a flight to Sydney and a second one to Taree, and as I entered the hospital room I saw Tracey in a bed which was surrounded by about twelve or more obviously grieving people; my former wife Kay, my two sons, daughter Kelly, and Tracey's partner Dave, were the only familiar faces in the room. After about an hour I finally had my turn to sit beside Tracey, who was in an induced coma.

As I looked at her lovely calm face I went into a state of intense bliss; it was unlike anything I had ever known before in my life. From my earlier Samapatti experiences and the Yoga sutras, I knew this was her state, not mine. I sat beside her for about twenty minutes, then the nurses suggested we go for a coffee because they were going to bathe Tracey and move her to another room. It was evening, and the others decided to go out for a meal. I opted to stay and had a coffee while I waited to sit beside Tracey again.

Sometime later, the nurses came and showed me to Tracey's room; it was a smaller room, and I sat beside her, watching the monitor screen beside her bed for five hours, noticing that her pulse was slowly increasing. Kay and Kelly came in around midnight and we sat there in silence. By now, Tracey's pulse had climbed above 200bpm and we watched it increase to over 300bpm, then it slowly decreased to 30 and stopped. That was about 1am.

We kissed Tracey and hugged each other. The nurses came in after a respectful wait, and we went to tell the others she had died. I was aware that Tracey had died within twelve hours of the time our 2-year-old son, Benjamin, had died 28 years earlier. It was just a twelve-hour difference, on the same day of the week, in the same month, when he had died, and both were buried on the same day of the week, at the same time of day. (For Kay and me it was ironic because their burial day was also the day of our wedding anniversary).

I flew home to Cecily, and the bliss stayed with me for almost three weeks; then it was gone. Oddly enough, one evening in the weeks after returning home from Taree, I was watching Cecily's choir group in a performance of Gilbert and Sullivan songs, and when Cecily's solo of *'Poor Wandering One'* began, the bliss returned during her solo performance and lasted one more day.

When we got home, I told Cecily about the bliss that came as I watched her sing, and I realised that my memory of that event, of Tracey's death, and the bliss, was only a simple narrative: 'this is what happened, when.' Thinking about my earlier memories, I realised that all of my memories have been like that; no emotion, no joy or pain, just this detached mental observation as a simple narrative.

At this point I began to understand a little more about Samapatti and knew I would have to do more than simply accept it; I needed to really understand what I didn't know about Patanjali's Yoga Sutras and everything else for that matter.

CHAPTER 3
Memory and Samapatti

In a general sense, we assume mind and memory to be normal functions of the brain and from that assumption we can include the belief that memory is triggered by the context of one's current thought as part of the mind. If this is true it might explain why western philosophers have rejected the Hindu model of consciousness, because the Hard Problem of consciousness insists that for any explanation of consciousness to be valid, it must incorporate the subjective aspect of the brain, from which consciousness arises, or words to that effect.

Culturally, we know this because our technology can demonstrate the correlation between measurable brain activity during an experience or medical procedure. All these measurements provide the basis for our brain atlas/mind maps, and out theory of mind and consciousness.

The Yoga sutras of Patanjali has a more explicit explanation for mind and consciousness and describes two kinds of memory; the first being the memory of an object or actual experience, and the second kind being the memory of something imagined or dreamt. It is not all bad though; Patanjali does supply a more complete description of mind and memory which I will describe in his words.

Patanjali's Yoga Sutra YS.1.11., and YS.1.41., also describe my kind of memory, but first let us consider the more familiar, 'first' kind of memory mentioned above, which is the kind 'normal' people experience. This sutra covers the subjective kind of memory and the subjective conscious mind so dear to the philosophers.

Included in Patanjali's description of the first kind of memory, is a process which includes 'modifications of the mind.' The term, modification of the mind, must be understood in the context of this specific Yoga Sutra, rather than western science's incomplete theory of mind, which I intend to explain later.

Patanjali's explanation of memory, YS. 1.11. states that:

"A cognition is associated with and coloured by the object of an apprehension and resembles and manifests the features of both the object apprehended and the process and instrument of apprehension. Such cognition then produces an imprint (samskara) that is similar to them both.

That samskara then manifests its identity with its own manifestative cause; it generates a memory.

This memory is identical in form to the same manifested identity and manifestative cause. It consists of both the object apprehended and the process and instrument of apprehension.

When the object of apprehension is primary, we call that memory. When the process and instrument of apprehension are primary, we call that intelligence."

What makes this difficult for the reader will be the terminology used by SVB, and I will address this as we go, beginning with the opening words of the Sutra. I can only write 'as if' my memory is like yours because I do not create a samskara as others do, and I will explain that crucial difference later on.

A cognition is the recognition of, or 'knowing,' of the object being remembered, *and is associated with and coloured by the object of an apprehension.* This means that my mind has recognised (captured or apprehended) the object and confirmed that I have known the object before. Therefore it becomes something I know; 'I know what it is because I remember when, where, how, and why, I know it.'

This memory is identical in form to the same manifested identity and manifestative cause. It consists of both the object apprehended and the process and instrument of apprehension. It is the same as you or I remembered it, (identity) but what is less obvious is that whatever has been recorded in my memory at an earlier time, and how it was recorded (manifestative cause) in my system, has remained in that system.

Such cognition then produces an imprint (samskara) that is similar to them both.

This tells us that a new configuration has been formed relative to this event, including the context of that event, time, place, how I felt then, and what I thought at the time. (in other words, it has 'modified' my mind to include any differences that may be related to the earlier context of knowing this object and its current context.

That samskara then manifests its identity with its own manifestative cause; it generates a memory. This means it has created a separate record of this event, so now I have two separate memories of this object or event to explain.

When the object of apprehension is primary, we call that memory.

This is how most people experience memory, we remember what one or more of our senses have experienced, as well as the Whom, How, What, When, Where, and Why, of my response.

"When the process and instrument of apprehension are primary, we call that intelligence (buddhi)."

This final sentence of YS. 1.11, is where our western model of mind would disagree with Patanjali, not because Patanjali or the western model is wrong; it is because this rarely happens. It is easy enough to accept consciousness entering at the first evolute as we see on the Yoga diagram, and buddhi can easily fit with the idea that the mind can discriminate between 'this' and 'that.'

The problem would surface in philosophy and psychology; in the current theory of mind, this discrimination should take place in the brain, which is physical matter, and that comes into play at the last evolute on the Yoga diagram, at the point where matter becomes atomic. Patanjali says discrimination happens at buddhi, which is at the first evolute on the diagram, and I will try to resolve this difference as we move through the book.

This Sutra also relates in part to YS 1.41., which is about the coalescence of two minds in Samapatti, as mine did with Tracey's mind in the event I described in the previous chapter, and in my experience with the cat and its dream of a garden. Samapatti is a different state of consciousness, and I will explain both of these Yoga sutras in this Chapter as we continue.

YS. 1. 41. states:

"When one's modifications have subsided, his (mind's) stability on and coalescence with the apprehender, the process and instrument of apprehension and the objects of apprehension, like pure crystal (which takes on the reflection and colour of proximate objects), is called Samapatti."

Now I will dissect this Sutra, YS. 1.41., in the same manner as before, noting that Samapatti is a different/higher state of consciousness to be explained later.

"When one's modifications have subsided, means that the observer has entered a Samadhi state, which effectively means that the *cognitive act of a person* seeing an object, or event, happens at the level of mahat/buddhi.

"her/his (mind's) stability on and coalescence with the apprehender, the process and instrument of apprehension and the objects of apprehension," means the person (seer) has the objectivity of buddhi and mahat, without the personal baggage of ego and memory.

"like pure crystal (which takes on the reflection and colour of proximate objects), is called Samapatti."

This means that what the seer experiences is *the subject's memory and manifestative cause* in the present momentary context, while the subject will experience *the seer's momentary context*. What may not be obvious to a reader is that the seer is only aware of the subject's mind because the seer's mind has been 'brought under control' i.e. it is not at Ahamkara; it is at the level of mahat/buddhi. The same is true of the subject, whose mind is under control by the seer's focus and will temporarily experience the seer's stillness as her/his own experience, meaning it becomes an actual memory for the subject as described in YS.1.11.

In the film about Bohm's life and ideas, Krishnamurti says that the observer is the observed, I think he should have added that the observed is also the observer. You, the reader, can get an idea of how this works in real life from the examples of the disturbed cat, and of my response to my daughter Tracey's mind when I sat beside her bed in the hospital at Taree.

I still have more to explain about the Yoga diagram, but it can be complicated enough with Sanskrit words and I think the best way to do that is to take the time to present it incrementally. To do that I will separate the information into a series of small steps which can relate to what I find from books about biophysics by biophysicists.

My mentor for some of those years, the late Dr Bevan Reid MD, was a cancer researcher at the University of Sydney, and he wrote the Foreword of my earlier book, *"Thinking on the other side of Zero[14],"* in which he suggests that 'to understand the way Oliver thinks, one must employ the imaginative number, *i*, the square root of minus1 (-1). Oddly enough, what he said is relevant here, but I will leave that aside for now and move on to chapter 3 to consider the Yoga diagram and its quantum transitions.

CHAPTER FOUR

Understanding
Patanjali's reality

In my search for an understanding of Patanjali's Yoga sutras, I looked for some references to the Vedas and found an interesting book by Bal Galangal Tilak, a contemporary of Mahatma Gandhi. Tilak was an extremely popular Indian academic and political activist in the 1930's who had been imprisoned by the British in India. At the time, the British needed Gandhi's political support in their negotiations with the Muslim leadership to form a representative Indian government, and Gandhi used his personal support to secure for Tilak the time and space to continue his research into the translation of the Vedas and other Hindu history.

Tilak's book, *"The Arctic Home in the Vedas[10],"* describes a culture living in the Arctic Circle, at a period estimated to be between 15,000 and 30,000 years ago. These people were living in a zone which was temperate at the time and had learned to cope with the six months of darkness by using this situation to study the night sky.

These people of the Arctic took advantage of the night sky uninterrupted by daylight and were able to recognise the fact the earth was rotating in its orbit around the sun, not the sun and moon rotating around earth. They saw that there was one star which remained overhead throughout the year, now known as the Pole Star.

The Vedic (Aryan) people also recognised that the end of the 6-month dark period coincided with the first appearance of what we know as the constellation of Orion, and made that date the beginning of their year, a time for celebration and festivities. They had developed a form of combinatorial mathematics, and through their observations recognised the seasons and the plane of the ecliptic.

They also developed an understanding of mind, which has formed the basis of the Vedas. It was Tilak's research into the Vedas which found a mathematical correspondence between astronomy, geographical location, and time, working out the time of when the constellation of Orion first appeared above the horizon to be in that place and date range, and their later observations of Orion, which confirmed the culture's journey south after the glaciation of the Arctic.

During their time in the Arctic these people developed their own technical language, Sanskrit, in part to describe what they learned about mind and the disciplines of science, philosophy, medicine, chemistry and mathematics. What is of interest in terms of this book are references to the Vedas, Upanishads, and other the related Vedic texts which inform Patanjali's Yoga sutras.

Of special interest here is the Sankhya Karika and I will discuss these observations which help me explain the basis of my experiences, and of Patanjali's mention of the physics throughout the sutras which has led me along this novel path. I refer to SVB's version of Patanjali's Yoga sutras[1], Samadhi Pada, which covers the first Chapter of the Yoga sutras, and introduces the reader or student to meditation and the Samadhi state.

In its INTRODUCTION, Swami Rama provides a diagram which describes that descent of consciousness into matter. Included in the commentary are references to Sankhya which, from my perspective, can benefit from modern interpretations or ideas, and I will describe my understanding of these ideas one by one.

The first idea I had about this was prompted by the statement, *'the ancient ones said that the smallest possible space is merely a point without mass,'* and I make a note of it here because in SVB's comments on Swami Rama's Yoga diagram, he tells us the diagram represents the *'descent of consciousness into matter.'*

The first inference here is that consciousness is external to, and significantly different from, matter, and the diagram shows that the unmanifested energy evolves into matter by a process which the diagram represents. From my perspective, this process is the reverse of Einstein's $E = MC^2$, which Patanjali tells us is a cyclic process of creating, sustaining, and dissolving. In western cultures creation is the sole domain of God the Creator. We rarely talk about the sustaining and dissolving aspects of this trinity, which relate to living and dying according to the will of God.

It is clear from the diagram that the process begins with Prakriti, and in SVB's overview of Sankhya, we find there are two eternally coexistent principles:

purusha: the conscious spiritual-energy principle
prakriti: the unconscious material-energy principle

The purusha principle is ever-pure, ever-wise, ever-free. It is that self (atman) which never comes into the trap of ignorance and bondage. It is only prakriti, activated like a magnet, which comes into association with purusha and receives his rays.

Prakriti is the unmanifest, intangible, subtlest origin of what later becomes tangible matter and consciousness. Prakriti consists of the equilibrium of the three gunas (attributes), described by Patanjali as:

Sattva: luminosity, purity, lightness, harmony, producing pleasure.

Rajas: activity, energy, movement, producing pain.

Tamas: dullness, inertia, darkness, stasis, producing stupor.

So long as the three gunas remain in perfect equilibrium, there is no universe. Only as disequilibrium occurs are the various phenomena called *vikaras* or *vikrtis,* modifications or evolutes, produced/created.

Sankhya believes in a theory of causation called *sat-karya-vada* whereby objects are not something new produced from any quanta other than those inherent in their causes. Nothing new is created: only the energies change form. The special attributes of a cause become manifest and tangible, given certain innate propensities of nature. Thus, what lay unmanifest within prakriti becomes manifest in its product (*vikrti*), the phenomenal universe, complete with all the evolutes or products within it.

All evolutes carry within themselves all three gunas and nothing exists that does not include all three gunas together. Variances in the nature of all phenomena, entities, attributes, self-identifications, tendencies, and inclinations, choices, personalities, relationships, and acts, all depend on the dominance and preponderance of gunas.

- where sattva dominates and is served by rajas and tamas, the manifestation appears sattvic in that manifestation.
- but where Tamas dominates, Tamas causes stagnation and dullness; Rajas struggles to change the status quo; and Sattva remains dormant, waiting to be energized with the help of Rajas.

This provides examples of the interdependence among the gunas. Rajas provides the constant oscillation and sattva and tamas produce a pull, each in its own direction, seeking to be dominant. The nature and acts of objects, phenomena, and entities, change as the equilibrium or balance of forces among the inherent gunas undergoes an alteration. Here the point to keep in mind is that all the evolutes are modifiable and can be modified further. Thus, there are twenty-three modifications produced from *the conscious spiritual-energy principle.*

SVB describes the Yoga diagram as *unfolding from Prakriti at the top into a descending series of evolutes, each of which submerge into the preceding cause from which it appeared; finally, all phenomena dissolve into prakriti. The cycles of creations and dissolutions, because of the inherent nature of prakriti, are endless.*

This is the process of 'the descent of consciousness into matter,' and it begins when Purusha's light illuminates Prakriti.

The reflection of Purusha produces its own image (on the unmanifested energy) which Patanjali calls purusha.

To understand this process from a modern perspective, what Patanjali has described in a metaphorical sense is the fundamental consciousness of Purusha as the seer in a Samapatti relationship with Prakriti, the subject. Within that same context, the unmanifested energy, prakriti (Prakriti illuminated), becomes *the unconscious material-energy principle,* which can be modified, and the attributes of prakriti which had been in a state of equilibrium before will be in a state of disequilibrium. This disequilibrium reflects the consciousness of purusha, which has become the seer in a Samapatti relationship with prakriti as its subject, and purusha 'knows' the mind of prakriti in this quantum moment.

Swami Rama's Yoga diagram

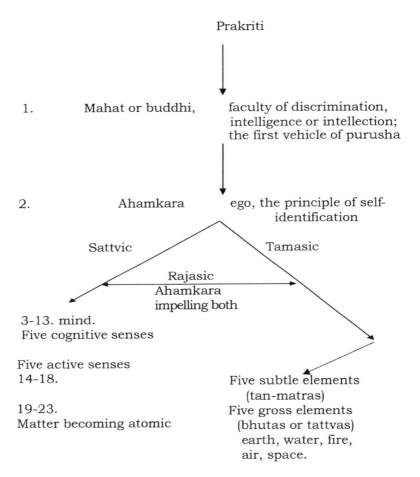

Fig. 4.1.

If one can be objective for a moment, it can be seen that the phrase, 'the reflection of Purusha on Prakriti' is the source of the belief about humans being created in the image of God, allowing us to claim superiority over all other living entities. What we don't recognise is that in Patanjali's Vedic reality, and in Bohm's Wholeness,

God has no 'distinguishing mark,' and certainly has no preference for humanity over the natural world.

In reference to the yoga diagram, I must explain that we will need to consider that, of all the gunas, it is rajas which produces each quantum moment by virtue of the fact that it is in fact an oscillation which is perpetually switching between sattva and tamas because Patanjali tells us that the cycles of creations and dissolutions are endless.

I will describe how that switching is achieved later, in chapter 5, and moreover, SVB tells us that every interaction on the diagram is referred to mahat, which shares evolute 1 with buddhi, the first vehicle of purusha.

Another attribute of mahat is that of having the title of the greatest teacher, a conundrum at least because that same title is attributed to 'space' as the final of the five gross elements at evolute 23 at the point where matter becomes atomic. The conundrum is resolved when we realise that the whole diagram is in the quantum domain of potential outcomes, which means that it is time asymmetric, allowing us to consider every interaction according to the nature of the conscious information without the impediment of time.

Thus, every interaction exists simultaneously *as the inherent nature of prakriti, meaning that the cycles of creations and dissolutions endless, and that the nature of every suite of guna attributes is already known by buddhi when an interaction is made.*

The interactions will always be between mahat and purusha's observation, buddhi, as a comparison of the current moment against the previous moment in a process of discriminating between the quantum information related to the observation made by purusha (Bohm's potentials/manifestative causes) within a quantum moment. In other essays I have considered buddhi's consciousness as purusha's observation and comparison against the previous moment to effectively be a 'quantum measurement' and I have related such measurements in terms of John Wheeler's[11,12] 'sum over histories' to highlight buddhi's access to the information related to the samskaras which create a memory. This information can also explain Bohm and Hiley's *hidden variables*[21] in the Implicate Order. Now, let us consider the process itself in the context of consciousness as it would present on the diagram as conscious information, mind, or memory.

Patanjali tells us that there is only one self: call it atman, Brahma, or God. What we know from chapter 2 is that there is a 'process and instrument of apprehension,' and we might assume this would be purusha, but this will be incomplete. We must factor in the ratio of the gunas present in the observation of some object being reflected upon by the conscious spiritual-energy principle.

In that observation there are aspects of Sattva, Rajas, and Tamas, which bring mind and ahamkara into the nature of the observation. What I mean is that identity/ego will always be part of the observer, making every observation a subjective one,

and SVB has taken this into account when he says that there is a degree of composite sentience (asmita) in the observation because the seer (in this case purusha), is in a Samapatti relationship, and 'knows' the observation from the perspective of the subject, which introduces the identity of the subject (ahamkara) into the conscious observation.

In YS.1.41, Patanjali says that asmita is the instrument of apprehension, and '*like pure crystal, becomes affected by the proximate object,*' which will be the mind field of the subject in the seer's observation. Therefore, asmita introduces all of the past experiences of the subject into every observation, which includes I am-ness, attraction, repulsion, fear of death and stupefaction.

This is where I must include all the knowledge I had gained from my Samapatti experiences and begin to build a clearer picture of what is meant by a conscious observation through the agency of asmita, 'the instrument of apprehension.'

To do this I will use the experience in which I observed the cat's experience in the Samapatti state. In the early 2000's I was fortunate enough to ask physicist, Professor Basil Hiley, how a physicist would describe my experience with the cat; he said the best word would be 'entanglement.'

Now, as I look back on that experience from Patanjali's perspective I can understand that the cat's response to Samapatti had been to change from its initial state of confusion and antisocial behaviour, (its own ahamkara) to my Samapatti state in which Sattva was dominant. This change is what Patanjali has called a *vikrti*, or modification of the mind, and for the cat this modification became a samskara which created a memory, the effect of which was to 'take on' that change as a new 'manifestative cause,' which changed in its subsequent behaviour to the perspective of a comfortable time in its life.

There was no change to the cat's identity because in that state I was the seer and therefore I was operating according to the conscious spiritual-energy principle. This different response to that experience, and to all the experiences I provided in chapter 2, is the natural outcome for anyone who is the seer in this Samadhi state.

What must be noted is that I experienced the cat's subjective mind at the time, but there was no samskara created of my subjective experience of the cat's mind field, and it illustrates what is missing in the enigma of mind and consciousness. I will explain this last point by repeating the relevant parts of Patanjali's explanation of memory sequentially and interpreting the process as it happens on the Yoga diagram.

I begin with my own explanation of YS. 1.11, which happens at evolute 1 on the diagram and I will assume this is the second kind of memory in which the object is being remembered by someone who is in a state of wakefulness.

A cognition is associated with and coloured by the object of an apprehension and resembles and manifests the features of both the object apprehended and the process and instrument of apprehension.

Such cognition then produces an imprint (samskara) that is similar to them both. For the cat, it was the imprint of an earlier time before its trauma.

That samskara then manifests its identity with its own manifestative cause; it generates a memory.

This memory is identical in form to the same manifested identity and manifestative cause. It consists of both the object apprehended and the process and instrument of apprehension.

When the object of apprehension is primary, we call that memory. When the process and instrument of apprehension are primary, we call that intelligence (buddhi).

A *cognition* refers to a moment of recognition or 'knowing,' of the object being remembered, *and is associated with and coloured by the object of an apprehension.* This means that purusha has recognised (captured or apprehended) the object and confirmed that the object before has been known before this observation. Therefore the cognition is the recognition *of something already known*; 'I know what it is because I remember when, where, how, whom, and why, I know it.'

This memory is identical in form to the same manifested identity and manifestative cause. It consists of both the object apprehended and the process and instrument of apprehension. It has the same identity you, I, or the cat remembered about it, but what is less obvious is that whatever has been recorded in memory at an earlier time, and how it was recorded (as manifestative cause) in this process, has remained in that process.

Such cognition then produces an imprint (samskara) that is similar to them both.

This tells us that a new configuration has been formed relative to this event, including the context of that event, time, place, how you, I, or the cat felt then, and what was thought at the time. In other words, it has 'modified' both minds to include any differences that may be related to the earlier context of knowing this object and its current context.

That samskara then manifests its identity with its own manifestative cause; it generates a memory.

This means it has created a separate record of this event, so now I have two separate memories of this object or event to explain, and the explanation is described by its subjective experience; the where, when, and how it felt, and why I know it.

"When the object of apprehension is primary, we call that memory."

This is how most people experience memory, we remember what one or more of our senses have experienced, as well as their response.

"When the process and instrument of apprehension are primary, we call that intelligence."

Here Patanjali is describing my experience of memory, in which, unlike your experience of memory, there is no samskara created by my experience, despite the fact that my experience was a subjective one when that experience happened. This is a salient point which, when fully understood can make a contribution towards developing a practical model of mind and memory based on this Samapatti experience and Patanjali's Yoga sutras.

The subjective component of all my Samapatti experiences are in fact my experience of the subject's mind because I was the seer in that Samapatti relationship where is the coalescence of two minds. My knowledge of the experience or event is 'intelligence;' not my intelligence per se, but meaning it is buddhi's reflection of purusha's observation, which is why it is not a subjective experience.

There is one further aspect I must mention here to dispel any idea that when I am in the role of seer I am in a special category. This is not so; my Samapatti is still connected to my personal identity, asmita, but there is no manifestative cause involved, and to that marginal extent I have a connection to the conscious spiritual-energy principle, purusha, which also has no samskara/manifestative cause.

If I can go back to the time of my febrile convulsions, the prolonged elevated temperature had effectively erased the neural connections related to the first four years of my life. This would include the sense of self as Alan, and this absence of self as Alan is what others hope to achieve through yoga and meditation. It is what 'established me in the Samadhi state.'

This time around I must go deeper into Patanjali's description of memory because I intend to explain this process as it operates on the Yoga diagram. I have earlier alluded to the diagram being a series of quantum interactions of information, and there are points I must cover before I start this discussion about my experience with the cat.

The first point to note is the difference between how your mind works and how my mind works in terms of mind and memory, and I begin with the experience of seeing an object. For you, the process begins with the awareness of the object which is primary in your process of cognition. You 'know' the object being recognised and your mind will create an identical object to produce a samskara which creates a memory and its associated manifestative cause which subsequently modifies the mind.

Now you have two identical memories of this object, each with its associated manifestative cause, the latest of which has given you the subjective experience of 'knowing' that object from the perspective of *the conscious spiritual-energy principle coloured by asmita*, which will have a contextual connection to your earlier memory of the object which gave you a similar subjective experience of the object.

My cognition of the same object would follow the first step in which I 'know' the object from the perspective of *the conscious spiritual-energy principle coloured by asmita seeing it*, but as I said earlier, I have no subjective experience of recognition. Later, when I remember that object, it is a conscious observation that comes from the perspective of purusha without asmita, as if it were an observation made by a dispassionate third person, leaving me with buddhi's observation that 'this is what happened when I saw this object.' I ask you, the reader, to join me in using the cat's experience as an example of Samapatti, and I will dissect my observation of that experience to have you develop an understanding of consciousness as a process.

The initial condition of the cat was one of pain and trauma from an older experience which had modified its mind to such an extent that it behaved the way its owner described as antisocial and unnatural, in that it had not washed itself in more than a year. These effects of the cat's trauma meant that it had this embedded manifestative cause, *samskara,* which I had experienced initially as a continuous series of mental images of flashing lights when I placed my hand on its head after the cat was placed on my lap and it went to sleep.

The reason the cat went to sleep is that its mind responded to my stillness, and its response was the 'modified manifestative cause' of going to sleep in a sense of comfort and safety; it remembered an earlier time before its trauma.

49

After sleeping for twenty minutes on my lap, the cat's flashing lights gave way to a quiet and familiar garden scene which I saw from the cat's perspective. This is an indication that my calmness was experienced by the cat, taking its mind back to an earlier time, (a manifestative cause), when its life was calm and familiar, which became a samskara which changed its manifestative cause yet again by modifying the cat's mind as it experienced my calmness.

After a further twenty minutes in this now familiar state the cat had begun the process of waking, which I knew 'intuitively' because of being in a Samapatti state where 'two minds coalesce' or become entangled. The cat woke up in this modified and now familiar state of an older memory. Its new memory was generated by its manifestative cause, part of which included earlier experiences, *'sum over histories,* of washing itself in moments of calmness and satisfaction. All my Samapatti experiences can be understood as iterations of the same process with only a change of subject in each case.

In his commentary on Samapatti in YS. 1. 41., Vyasa says, the mind is like a pure-born crystal. The purusha, the senses and the elements are respectively the agent, the instruments, and objects of apprehension. The mind-field's 'stability on and coalescence with' them means that it remains concentrated on them and takes on their form. This is called proficiency, transmutation, coalescence and attainment of the given state of consciousness.

Vyasa's comment on Samapatti can be seen as a summation of the process of consciousness in a Samapatti relationship, which had the effect of the cat (subject) taking on the purusha, and the senses elements of the agent (seer), the instruments and objects of apprehension.

At the same time I took on the cat's consciousness, and the senses elements, of the agent (cat), its instruments and objects of apprehension,' giving me the cat's experience of the flashing lights and mental confusion. This is exactly the same process in every one of my Samapatti experiences given in Chapter 2, and I believe it can account for philosophy's lack of a viable explanation of the subjective component of mind and consciousness.

CHAPTER 5

The Process of Quantum Transitions

This process involves information in the unmanifested zero-point energy through a series of quantum interactions. SVB explains that the first word in the first yoga sutra, YS 1.1., is *atha*, which translates in English as 'now.' It also means 'a transition' or change, and the transition relates to the information and context in one quantum moment to the information and context of an earlier or next moment. To quote SVB,

Each moment arises directly from infinity.
Each moment dissolved into infinity.
The next moment arises directly from infinity.

Concentration on what is between the dissolution of the prior moment and the arising of the subsequent moment opens the gateway to infinity. SVB brings even more clarity in his commentary when he points out there is more in the transition than a beginning of the conversation. The transition between these two sets of quantum information (manifestative cause), can be understood to be part of the moment's context, and the discrimination between each moment and its related context is what Patanjali tells us is the intelligence and intellection at the first evolute on the yoga diagram as a faculty of purusha, the conscious observer.

I consider the yoga diagram to be a separate way of explaining something which, for the layperson, is a complex model of reality with no conscious or subjective reference component, an enigma. It will become especially useful when considering subjects such as the fundamental process which I employ to describe the creation of mind, memory, and consciousness. It is also the same process underpinning the creation of matter, in which one finds this reality to be cyclic rather than a simple, straight-forward one-off event enacted by a benevolent creator.

Now, before I lose you with a flood of challenging terms such as the cyclic universe, religious or science perspectives, and outcomes, quantum information, zero-point energy, spacetime asymmetry, and the like, I had better come back to your manifested world to unravel these off-the-cuff generalisations before we get around to reconsidering the diagram on page 49.

In the Vedas we find the word, Satchitananda, which represents the original trinity concept; Creating, Sustaining and Dissolving, and if we consider that three-step cycle we find it represents every living form as well as the whole physical cosmos, and we need to keep that trinity in mind in this exploration of reality.

Patanjali and SVB use terms similar to those used by the ancient ones, but these are terms foreign to us, and I will explain the first one we will come across in SVB's narrative. 'Without distinguishing mark,' is a term we don't find in general conversation today, but it is important here because it is used to make a distinction between two simultaneous observations, one observation is that of purusha as the conscious spiritual-energy principle, and the other observation is that of buddhi, inferred as having the composite sentience of asmita added to buddhi . To explain this last point, I refer to SVB's explanation of Patanjali's yoga sutras, Samadhi Pada, in which a student is introduced to the Samadhi state.

Included in SVB's commentary are references to Sankhya, which, from my perspective, can raise modern interpretations or ideas, and I will describe these one by one because I believe they can make the science in Sankhya relevant to what most of us know in a general sense.

The first reference I find is the statement, 'the smallest possible space is merely a point without mass,' and I consider this to correspond with Patanjali's description of the word, 'space,' as the final of the 'gross elements' at evolute 23 at the bottom of the Yoga diagram. I must explain the description given for that 'space,' because it differs from our accepted understanding of physical space. This 'special space' is known as Akasha and has the title of The greatest teacher. That same title is applied to Mahat at evolute 1, and from that 'coincidence we learn that Mahat has access to the same information *in the same moment in the process.* In today's physics it can be recognised as a similar space in physics, defined as the Planck length of 10^{-33}cm., albeit for a different reason, given a time difference of hundreds or thousands of years.

My conclusion is that Akasha is quantum information in the unmanifested state. As I think about this unmanifested state, I ask myself what could manifest in this state, and from the yoga diagram it is consciousness that will manifest as mind and does this through the same process used to manifest matter.

For me, the presence of a process resonates with Bohm's concept of Wholeness and the Implicate Order in which information as a quantum potential, manifests or 'unfolds' from an unmanifested state. From my limited knowledge of physics, the only existing description of a process capable of being described as manifesting matter is Einstein's equation, $E = MC^2$, which suggests to me that Einstein's equation is about matter manifesting (creation) when energy is transformed in what must be a fundamental process, and unmanifesting within that same process.

Returning to the idea of that fundamental process described in the yoga sutras, I can say it has been written in a form that infers a spiritual perspective, with an occasional mention of the physics of Sankhya. For the process to have the capacity to manifest matter 'out of nothing,' and to unmanifest that matter back into 'nothing' within the same process, suggests to me that the information in space must be intelligent and active in a manner akin to what we call AI (Artificial Intelligence).

The physics of this AI is evident in G Srinivasan's (GS), Sankhya Karika[5], in which he says that the information in a singularity is *'coherent, perpetual, dynamic and unmanifest'*. When I apply this rule to the information in space, I find it to be conscious memory which Patanjali tells us is active (as the Greatest Teacher) and unmanifest, which places it in Akasha. Moreover, it can be interpreted as purusha, the conscious spiritual-energy principle.

This last point means that this active intelligence aspect of Akasha is available at every point on the yoga diagram, and I see that availability of this active intelligence as a selective (conscious) quantum entanglement is the fundamental process which manifests mind and matter from 'nothing', and unmanifests that same mind and matter into 'nothing' to become a singularity.

I have assumed Einstein had zero-point energy in mind when he coined his eponymous equation, $E = MC^2$, but I still must account for MC^2, which I think can be the five *gross elements* evolving from the five *subtle elements* on the bottom right-hand side of the diagram. My thoughts go back to the yoga sutras where Patanjali tells us that the whole reality is cyclic on a cosmic scale, rather than the spiritual model, which assumes creation to be a one-off event, which came from 'nothing' through the agency of a benevolent creator.

What the cosmic model suggests to me is that the process is two-fold, in that matter manifests from a quantum potential, and returns to the unmanifested state as 'nothing,' *plus the information accrued from its momentary experience in the manifested state.* From my meagre understanding of physics, I can say that this cycling between the manifested and unmanifested states could come from the collapse of a galaxy/or galaxies into a black hole, the end point of which is a singularity.

When I consider this singularity in terms of Patanjali's yoga diagram, I find that Akasha itself can be better understood as a singularity, but Akasha also infers accessible information, a notion seriously at odds with Stephen Hawking's Information Paradox[20], in which Hawking says that 'nothing can escape from a black hole, not even information'.

I can offer an option of obtaining the information related to a singularity without any challenge to Hawking's paradox[20]. From my perspective, the answer can be that the information in the singularity relates to the quantum information being defined as an imaginary number, *i,* to denote it as <u>conscious quantum potential information</u>, entangled with this 'point without mass.'

This point without mass will include all the information present in the spacetime occupied by the matter throughout the entire formation of that matter, preceding and during, the event that became the black hole. I can be out on a philosophical limb here, but for Akasha to be a singularity complete with retained information, one must assume the singularity can be capable of holding information *one way or another.*

Looking again to what Patanjali has said about that last point, directly or indirectly, in this statement about Akasha containing: *"All the knowledge that has ever been known in the past, is currently known, and will be known in the future, can be known now by a person in the Samadhi state,"* I find that Patanjali is saying, unambiguously, that a singularity holds conscious information.

The yoga diagram is about consciousness 'descending into matter,' and in that last paragraph I assume that consciousness relating to 'knowing' in this context means the information is consciously active, which, from my perspective confirms the nature of all information in Akasha. Bohm and Hiley mention active information and given that the yoga diagram can be understood to be quantum information in the unmanifested state, I believe active information infers quantum interactions (activity) between the evolutes on the yoga diagram.

Therefore, if one can think of the yoga diagram in a context of quantum interactions, substituting Bohm's potentials for the Sanskrit terms on the yoga diagram can be seen as a process in which momentary quantum entanglements can create matter. The fact of active conscious information in this 'special space' of Akasha at the final evolute on the diagram, is the context of 'information as potential' which Bohm had wanted to explain. It can also support Bohm's thoughts about Einstein's relativity.

Now, we can take another look at Einstein's equation and think what MC^2 might mean in a practical sense. $E = MC^2$ may seem familiar to us because it has been familiar from our time in secondary school, but if I look at it from the perspective of 'E' being unmanifested energy, what does 'zero-point energy' mean in relation to the creation?

To answer that question, we need to realise that with this equation, Einstein is explaining that energy is matter in a different form, be that a solid, liquid, gaseous, *or unmanifested,* and to achieve that transition from the unmanifested form of energy to matter and vice versa, we must multiply matter M, for manifestation of energy from matter, or divide energy E, by Einstein's factor of C^2 to manifest matter from energy.

From my own understanding of Patanjali's yoga sutras, I will say (with tongue in cheek) that the Einstein factor M is Patanjali's *'manifestative cause,'* without any need for Einstein's use of C^2. This has Patanjali's manifestative cause/samskara translated into physics as consciously active quantum information, to be understood as an imaginary mathematical expression, in a process, also an imaginary mathematical expression which translates in everyday language as Creating, Sustaining and Dissolving.

I never did find out what the relationship was between Einstein's M and the speed of light because I was young at the time, and accepted what I was taught, and I remembered what I had been taught because I realised that it would eventually be an answer to a question in an exam. What I learned from Patanjali is that consciousness, like Einstein's energy, can experience transformations too, all of which emanate from the same 'nothing,' mentioned in religion.

In Einstein's equation, C^2 is the speed of light squared, which becomes a large multiplier in comparison to M, the matter in question. If M stands for a kilogram of uranium, our imagination may liken it to the energy released in an atomic explosion, but is this how we should be thinking if we want to explain what is meant by C^2 in terms of an electron, an electrical field, or the Higgs boson?

If we are to consider a theoretically fundamental process which can produce energy, matter and/or consciousness, Einstein's equation is not going to lead us to consciousness or matter being created from 'nothing,' and here my point is that matter is created from a form of energy which is a quantum potential, and that potential is what Bohm's Wholeness and Implicate Order is all about because for Bohm, the 'Order' is a potential, *Implicit throughout the whole.* Consciously active might be an appropriate alternative for Implicit.

The way Bohm and Hiley described this 'order' was to use the analogy of a hologram, in which any point within the hologram has the potential to create the complete hologram. From my perspective, the potential for the whole hologram to be *Implicit* in every point of the hologram, the potential must be its whole manifestative cause, a quantum potential, *i,* which suggests to me that Patanjali's yoga sutras can fulfil Bohm's need for an explanation of wholeness to be found 'from outside of physics.' Not necessarily from outside of physics at all, but from an entangled unimagined perspective.

To digress for a moment to address the issue of the imaginary number, *i,* being the square root of *minus 1.* It can only be used as a real number if we imagine *the quantum potential in the unmanifested energy to be described as minus 1, i.e., 'on the other side of zero,'* and the manifested form of that potential as 1, because the quantum potential has become realised.

Therefore, the entanglement of these two forms of the energy is 1 multiplied by minus 1 as an entanglement, *and the square root of that entanglement will be* √-1. (I remember from my time as a radio technician, √-1 was used to denote *j,* in calculations related to alternating current in electrical circuits).

Patanjali's sutras Ys 1.11., and YS.1.41., are currently 'outside of physics' when describing the process of memory and Samapatti, yet they have introduced us to the terms of 'manifestative cause,' 'the process and instrument of apprehension' and 'modifications of the mind.' In many respects, all these terms are comfortably 'outside of physics,' while simultaneously capable of being understood from a novel perspective of physics.

Dare I say it? What Patanjali's yoga sutras have in common with physics is Bohm's Wholeness and the Implicate Order. Einstein's equation is there too if one looks carefully, and I will start with that commonality first because what is common in creating matter from nothing is Patanjali's 'unmanifested energy,' which is the form of the energy that Einstein referred to as E, which is the amount of energy in matter, expressed mathematically as MC^2.

If I consider this equation in terms of Wholeness, it must be true for a kilogram of coal, for a sun, a galaxy, and for a singularity if we want to consider everything, even the creation of matter or for life from 'nothing.' This is the same 'nothing' which, in quantum terms has a specific 'starting condition' for a fundamental quantum interaction that can produce matter and consciousness.

This starting condition of a quantum interaction is a singularity, which the ancient ones described as being 'merely a point without mass,' and to find such a point I could use its equivalent from physics: the Planck length of 10^{-33}cm. In that context though, I prefer to employ terms such as infinity because Patanjali says this point without mass is the smallest possible point, and from that perspective, $1/\infty$ is such a point.

Patanjali tells us that the universe is cyclic, meaning that systems in the cosmos are created from nothing, are sustained for a period, and dissolve back into nothing. The period of their existence can be nanoseconds or billions of years, but everything follows the same basic cycle. The last part fits the concept of matter in a black hole dissolving back into nothing, and when applied to Einstein's equation, the result is the E in that equation, which represents mass returning to become unmanifested energy, or in physics terms, zero-point energy, which I can quantify as $1/\infty$, without any spacetime dimensions or distinguishing marks for locality.

What Patanjali does not tell specifically us is that in the process of collapsing matter transforming into energy, the information related to all spacetime, and the quantum information observed by purusha throughout the existence of the former matter must be related to that process. What he does tell us quite specifically is that *all the spacetime related to the former matter which has become a singularity is called Akasha, the greatest teacher, and that all the information that has ever been known in the past, is currently known, and can be known in the future,* can be accessed in that Akashic space by someone in the Siddhi state. That information *is* the potential Bohm said would be present in his Implicate Order.

As I think about this unmanifested zero-point energy, I can understand that it has become part of, or indeed the context of a quantum event which, according to my understanding of Bell's theorem, now holds all the past spacetime information of experience entangled within that unmanifested energy. I have no intention of challenging Stephen Hawking's Information Paradox[20], and in any event, the singularity in question is not any black hole, but this 'former black hole' which precipitated the quantum entanglements just mentioned.

To explain this, I will give Patanjali's account of how consciousness 'descends into matter.' I will use the yoga diagram to help me explain this fundamental process as I understand it to be. Readers must shift from their familiar concept of reality to imagine this yoga diagram as a quantum process happening at a point with the dimension of 'nothing,' and having *quantum informational* inputs from the wholeness of infinity.

Above the diagram is Prakriti, the unmanifested energy that holds the fundamental potential for matter and consciousness. I also see Bohm's implicate order as this fundamental potential, and as the

MC^2 I talked about earlier because Prakriti is that special 'nothing', a singularity. There is another aspect of this fundamental potential, and that is the entangled quantum information at every nonlocal point of nothing throughout what will become 'real' spacetime. The other unknowns here are the two eternally coexistent principles, described in SVB's yoga sutras.

purusha, the conscious spiritual-energy principle, and
prakriti, the unconscious material-energy principle.

I will explain these principles step-by-step as they relate to evolute 1, mahat or buddhi, on the diagram.

The first point to explain is SVB's explanation in which there is a change from upper case P for Purusha and Prakriti to lower case p, and what we find is that when Purusha's light of consciousness reflects on or illuminates Prakriti, which is unmanifested energy MC^2, the reflected light, purusha, takes part in the transition from a quantum potential to a genuine experience in the material world, prakriti.

At this point I need to make a clear distinction between self, as absolute, and non-self as the individual self. This is where the diagram becomes confusing for some because the distinction comes from the fact that the quantum moments between self and non-self are time asymmetric, but before I explain that one, I need to explain absolute self. Not a challenging task if one has an objective outlook, and my analogy for that moment is the moment of conception in a general sense, without the spiritual viewpoint.

For a successful conception to be achieved, ovum and sperm must be living entities in that moment, and having accepted this brutal fact, I am saying that it does not mean a new life has begun; it is simply the case of the ovum being 'cloned.' The process of cloning the soon-to-be-mother begins when the ovum has been surrounded by a number of sperm, only one of which the ovum has accepted to become absorbed, causing a modified clone of the ovum to grow in the woman's uterus during what we call the period of gestation.

This embryonic clone is nourished and managed as part of the mother's body and mind (for the moment I will use mc²), and for that reason it is still part of the mother's body until the umbilical is cut and tied securely after the infant's birth.

For the benefit of the doubters, imagine if the soon-to-be-mother were stranded in a remote place and the placenta ruptured it is plausible that mother and child could bleed to death because there is only one blood supply. From that hypothetical perspective, *the embryo is an integral part of the soon-to-be-mother's body.*

The embryo's gender is decided by a process which has incorporated a combination of the DNAs of the sperm and ovum, and this combination changes the mother's DNA to match that of the embryo to prevent rejection by the mother's immune system and repeats for each subsequent embryo.

The embryo's mc² will be in a quantum entanglement with the mother's mc² and the father's mc² from this point forward, and the mother's mind is also connected to the infant at the Siddhi level of Samadhi known as 'intuition'. Note here that the infant's mind learns its name and family relationship during the years second to third years since its birth, and consciously becomes an individual entity separate from its mother, who is still the seer in the entanglement established with the embryo at conception, which accounts for her intuition and any post-natal depression in that trying time she endures alone because no other person shares her reality of the entanglement. For many, her depression is not easily understood, and from the perspective of others it is an enigma beyond their comprehension, accounting for even more depression for the mother because she intuitively knows they cannot understand this intuitive state.

This intuitive connection between the mother and the embryo, which is to become a separate individual after birth, is why a reasonable mind can respect the mother's sovereign right to her decision to either continue with the gestation or abort it. Such a decision is never a whim on the part of the mother-to-be; it a decision reached in the siddhi state that most of her critics will never access. It is from that perspective I consider any attempt to oppose this sovereign right of any woman is the ultimate form of personal violence against women. Its opposite, the support for a decision of this magnitude, is the compassion found at a level most of us can only wish for.

Taking this conception back to the two individuals' own conceptions which gave rise to their lives and subsequent ovum and the sperm, it should be obvious that life in each of their conceptions has been a continuation of the same life in their parents, which was present in the related sperm and ovum of this conception, making the model valid all the way back to the first appearance of life on this planet. The conclusion here is that there is one continuous life, lived in every individual form, which is why Patanjali tells us there is just one self, and has given that self the name, atman.

Atman is the collective name for every form of life, animal, and vegetable, which is impossible to isolate as an identifiable form, and therefore, represents the whole of life as a potential/context, and I can understand it as being part of Bohm's wholeness. Considering life from that perspective, I can say atman, in terms of every form of life is undefinable to the point of being 'without distinguishing mark,' and its collective conscious experience is Brahman, God, etc.

This idea of being 'without a distinguishing mark,' can be a distraction when we come to consider that we are all part of atman's collective of conscious experience, an element of which happens to be Einstein's MC^2, and this takes us back to Patanjali's 'manifestative cause.' If MC^2 is the fundamental manifestative cause in Bohm's concept of wholeness, then I propose using mc^2 as the individual manifestative cause and the process and instrument of apprehension of an individual memory and Samapatti as described in the yoga sutras.

With this fundamental point filed away but kept in mind, we can return to considering the yoga diagram from the individual perspective of ahamkara, ego. Thus, when this individual living form is in the presence of Purusha's reflected light, purusha, that form will become conscious in that quantum moment. This is a significant point the reader must note because here we need to understand that the individual living form is the subject in all the Samapatti quantum interactions existing at buddhi, and every interaction will draw of Wheeler's 'sum over histories' for its intuitive outcome.

On the yoga diagram, the individual form is in the presence of purusha, who is the seer in this Samapatti experience, and from this I can say the individual becomes conscious through this quantum entanglement of buddhi and purusha's reflection in a quantum interaction. These moments of quantum interaction are spacetime-asymmetric, which means that this individual living form becomes the momentary individual conscious form which I called mind, mc^2.

What has changed is that this conscious mind appears across the whole yoga diagram to manifest as an individual living form in every cell of that individual, each cell with its own expression of the gunas as ego, ahamkara, I-am-this-self as an individual personality, with the awareness of this quantum moment known by the individual mind and kept as a momentary individual memory as described by

Patanjali in YS1.11. The inclusion of that momentary memory is what Patanjali calls a samskara, 'a modification of the mind.'

What has not changed is that the memory of this moment is kept by MC^2, mentioned by SVB as *'every aspect of what was known in the past, is currently known, and what will become known in the future, already exists, and can be known at any time by anyone in the Samadhi state'*, as the universal memory, Akasha.

On the Yoga diagram, the significant point here is that the reader should note, is that MC^2 shares the same consciousness of buddhi, and the word 'apparently' becomes definitive in respect of understanding the diagram because Patanjali is telling us there is only one observer, purusha. This means that MC^2 is the manifestative cause of the whole. But the observation has a second aspect of composite sentience, asmita and I propose lowercase mc^2 applies an individual manifestative cause to the individual living form because buddhi is in the presence of ahamkara/ego.

So, once again we must take asmita into account as we consider the yoga diagram, where the first evolute on the diagram is mahat/buddhi, and the question a reader may ask is, what does 'mahat/buddhi,' mean? SVB tells us mahat is 'the universal buddhi, a small spark of which is the individual buddhi,' which is the first vehicle of purusha, the faculty of discrimination, intellection, and intelligence.

I found in SVB's description of the diagram, that every point on the diagram is referenced against mahat, and this resonated with what I had read in Sankhya Karika[5] by (GS). In that book I found that mahat is the pause between successive phases of the permanent oscillations, which occur as a spherical standing waveform through the expansion and contraction of the fundamental energy in the singularity. In my view, this description from GS corresponds with the moments of equilibrium and disequilibrium of the unmanifested energy, with mahat's pause being a moment of equilibrium which I equate to SVB's equilibrium of the gunas.

To understand why all the quantum interactions are referenced to mahat, we must go back to the momentary reflection of Purusha on Prakriti by atman, the manifestative cause MC^2, which appears at evolute 1 as buddhi, which reaches mind at evolute 12, and the subtle and gross elements at evolutes 14-18, and 19-23, respectively. I have already said that buddhi at this point in the process is in the presence of asmita, and this means that every quantum interaction at mahat/buddhi, *'a small spark of which is the individual buddhi,' Ahamkara.*

This is really significant because it is where we can differentiate between MC^2 and mc^2. Patanjali tells us that Samadhi is the natural state of consciousness/purusha, 'without distinguishing mark.' This provides me with a way to explain that difference, between Samadhi with seed and Samadhi without seed, the former being Samadhi with seed (Ahamkara the identity of the individual) plus its samskaras and manifestative cause, mc^2, and the latter being the Siddhi state, such as Samapatti, MC^2; without distinguishing mark, in this case the reflection of the consciousness purusha.

Thus, we have the purpose of yoga, which is to reach the state of our natural essence, the pure consciousness of purusha.

My view is that the term, manifestative cause, includes the mind, the five senses, the five subtle elements and the five gross elements, all of which are kept in Akasha as the Implicit Order with respect to the nonlocal space as well as spacetime, accounting for the déjà vu experiences, which some people have from time to time.

The one déjà vu experience that I remember came when my former wife Kay and I were having dinner with friends; after the meal, one friend asked me about Ouija boards, and I said we could try out our own version to see what comes through. We tore pieces of paper to represent the alphabet, setting the letters to create a circle about 50 centimetres in diameter. We placed an empty glass in the middle of the circle with each of us lightly placing one finger on the glass.

After a minute, the glass moved from letter to letter, spelling out sentences which said it was my brother Gordon making contact, explaining he and his wife were in a sailing boat he had built. At the time I didn't know Gordon had built this boat.

At the time, Gordon and his wife were sailing his boat at night, caught in a wild storm off the coast of Queensland and were trying to reach a safe harbour. The whole Ouija board incident only lasted for about 15 minutes, and we enjoyed the fun at the time as a simple game. Some years later, I met up with Gordon and he told me about that same event, and when I asked for the month and year of his experience it corresponded to the same time, month, and year, and in the same part of the Queensland coast described in our Ouija board game. Spooky action-at-a-distance.

Mind knows the information present in the momentary reflection at buddhi, and when we remember that mahat and buddhi are entangled, it can be obvious that at the end of that quantum moment, mahat becomes a new pause, the quantum equivalent of making a measurement, which will also have the same effect on buddhi. As buddhi and mahat are entangled, taking a measurement on mahat will effectively switch to the next observation by purusha at buddhi.

This is where buddhi's discrimination and intelligence comes to the fore and it 'knows' through purusha's consciousness what has changed. This momentary change is known across the whole diagram and supplies input to mind and body through the two limbs of the diagram, resetting the activities of the senses and the neural network.

SVB tells us that in the entanglement of mahat and buddhi there is a composite sentience that includes the presence of the reflection of purusha, and that this presence is called asmita (reflected spirit plus matter). It is asmita which is the instrument of apprehension and has the idea of self, albeit the self as in purusha, plus the notional self as in, ego, I am-ness. It is the presence of a notional self that brings identity to the object of observation, that same I am-ness, which is mc^2 and MC^2; therefore, the mind is defined by ahamkara, 'I am this body', the non-self.

Putting this another way, mc^2 becomes the 'individual mind', which identifies with the individual body-mind across the whole diagram. The relationship between MC^2 and mc^2 is the Samapatti state, in which MC^2 is the seer and mc^2 is the subject. I am aware this statement will be a difficult for the reader, but remembering GS and his description of MC^2 as *coherent, perpetual, dynamic and unmanifest*, I think it is reasonable to understand that coherent in this context is GS telling us that the information switching moment-by-moment (by Rajas on the diagram) in step with the equilibrium and disequilibrium of the gunas is the same step-by-step *coherent, perpetual, dynamic and unmanifest* oscillation in the unmanifest energy of prakriti.

Remember, Krishnamurti told us that the observer is the observed, and what this means is that in Samapatti, mc^2 and MC^2 coalesce; in other words, each mind is coloured by the other mind and vice versa. The effect is such that each 'becomes the other.'

If the reader thinks back to my examples of my experience in Samapatti, the lady with the leg fracture 'saw' in her mind what I had only thought. Similarly, I had the cat's experience from the cat's perspective, of being in a familiar garden. For the lady, and for the cat, each mind was 'modified' by what the other mind had as a genuine experience. For me, there was no modification of my mind because I was the seer in this Samapatti Samadhi state. I concede this absence of a modification on my part takes the discussion into the tricky question of what consciousness is; in fact, it serves to supply a finer degree of understanding of what consciousness is, and to explain that finer point I go back to evolute 1, 'mahat or buddhi', and the role of buddhi as first vehicle of purusha.

This 'first vehicle of purusha,' buddhi, is where we can understand that the consciousness of purusha (through its own coalescence as the subject in the primary Samapatti) is, the seer, and is able to know the experience of ahamkara without any modification, which leaves purusha equally unmodified and, 'without distinguishing mark.' What is also clear, at least in this whole thought experiment, is that consciousness itself can be understood (at the level of purusha and of an individual) to be separate from the body, which suggests to me that it is timeless, endless, immutable, and whole, which is what David Bohm wanted to explain.

The 'manifestative cause' is what I want to examine to find whether there is a plausible reason for the substitution of C^2 for something that is really the means of the transition from one form of matter into energy and vice versa, because this transition can surely work in both directions. This is how I understand consciousness through what Patanjali explained in the yoga sutras; in simple terms, there are various levels of consciousness, those in which the mind is modifiable, and those in which the mind is under the control of the something that remains unmodified.

To answer my own question, I will consider C^2 from the perspective of creation in the spiritual version of the diagram, and what I find is that creation in this spiritual context infers it is Brahman, or God, who 'creates' from 'nothing'. Looking at the yoga diagram again, I can see that it is Purusha that creates, and the only term mentioned that is closest to 'nothing' is Akasha, mentioned in Patanjali's description of the smallest space, which he says is merely 'a point without mass.'

This not a description of matter but of Bohm's potential for matter, and I can say that C^2 is the *potential for matter* part of the 'manifestative cause,' mentioned in chapter 2. Now I will move on to chapter 5 to think about how these fits with Sankhya in Bohm's concept of wholeness.

CHAPTER 6

The Enigma We Call God

I acknowledge the difficulty facing a normal person reading this book because I faced the same difficulty in trying to understand how the way I thought could be different from the way my colleagues thought. It has become clear to me that what my colleagues find difficult is the outcome I reach from the same starting point in a conversation, inferring that I use the process in a unique way or from a unique perspective.

From the beginning of drafting this book, I realised I would need to write incrementally about this enigmatic aspect of consciousness, which is why I don't expect a reader to have understood all of what I have written up to now, and I know more is needed to complete the whole picture.

I must continue making step-by-step references to some of the points already mentioned because that is how I learned to understand it myself. The experiences I shared with you earlier will have challenged the assumptions you may have made about mind, memory, and consciousness. I had to learn from the experiences of my subjects, and I believe you can learn from those experiences too if you can set aside the idea that I am saying your accepted reality is incomplete. I don't have a different reality, only an unfamiliar perspective of the whole reality.

From my perspective of the yoga sutras, Patanjali, and the teachers before him have explained the way to reach an understanding of the existence of God, not as an intangible enigma one can only know and trust implicitly through having an unshakable faith in God, but through the direct tangible experience of God's presence.

Not to be in that presence to the extent that one realises one's union with God, which is the ultimate Samadhi state of Kaivalya. A state in which one has recognised that the observer and the observed is the true Self's own essence. No, I mean being one in that Samadhi state who has realised the distinction between our mind and body, and the consciousness we all enjoy as living entities. There is a lot we can learn about an experientially known reality, rather than the illusion we have that consciousness and mind exist in a material form, through which one can only know God as an enigma.

What follows from that enigmatic definition is the need to challenge the process of thinking from GS's perspective of the Sankhya philosophy and science in the yoga sutras, in which the information in a quantum moment is associated to the moment prior and will evoke the potential information related to the next moment as a future quantum potential.

What leads an individual to have problems stemming from this process is that asmita (ignorance) brings to buddhi (purusha's conscious observer) an identity of self/ego, into one's future moment, which is unbidden and not consciously planned by this ego-self. The best way I can describe this problem to a normal person is to use the description in the yoga sutras, where the process is always a simple one of Concentration, Contemplation, Samadhi.

I can only explain the yoga sutras from my own perspective, which, by its very nature is foreign to many readers because I lack their subjective view of reality, and all I can know comes from the way I experience my version of memory when I appear to think about the experiences rather than remember them. My kind of memory was the last point in Patanjali's description of memory in YS 1.11, where it is simply called intelligence, because it has no samskaras, and therefore, it has no memory, per se, or manifestative cause. This is why my memory/recall is a conscious narrative, of the experience from a third person perspective.

The central theme in Patanjali's yoga sutras is wholeness, and in many respects, I can see a connection between Bohm's wholeness and Einstein's relativity, the latter which Bohm sought but had not found, and I will get back to Einstein in a little while.

A defining aspect of Purusha is the recurring theme of being 'without distinguishing mark,' and some of it can be thought of as what sets Purusha/God apart from us, but that is an illusion.

Vyasa's commentary on YS.1.11, begins with the words, 'A cognition arises', which tells me that every memory is a conscious observation by purusha, and what this explains is that all the information we experience as memory will be conscious information, and conscious in this context for most normal people is sensory; that is, it will have the sensory aspects of emotion, touch, taste, smell, vision, and sound. This is why I, in the Samadhi state, experienced what the cat 'felt' about the 'garden' in its dream, and why/how I later knew the cat would wake up.

It is why psychics and mystics, mostly, mostly male, experience information consciously from a male perspective, giving rise to the belief that 'God' is male, and why female mystics or psychic women have experienced 'God' as a Goddess.

In this context of human intelligence, I want to challenge how and what we humans can think. Because we are humans, we think we have more intelligence than plants and animals, and that is a dangerous way to think. As life forms without a superior being, plants and animals have what we have in terms of being conscious;

the only difference is how their consciousness manifests. Remember my experience with the cat; I 'knew the garden was familiar' and I knew that the familiarity was known consciously in the cat's mind, not mine. So let us check out how reality works for them and us too.

The yoga diagram in chapter 3 does not apply exclusively to humans in the spiritual sense or in a Sankhya science sense. I assume this to be true because SVB said that without the gunas, the universe would not exist, meaning that the universe manifests as the direct result of a universal manifestative cause. The attributes Patanjali noted for each guna remains the same for plants and animals as those we have imagined applied exclusively to humans; anyone who has a pet, or a garden, or has had the misfortune to or hand-feed lions, surf, or swim in known Great White shark territory will recognise that what I have said is true.

To explain further, in view of the omni-characteristics of Purusha, I can say that purusha is the reflection of Purusha's light on Prakriti, which means all the characteristics of Purusha, including consciousness and the knowledge of self is present at evolute 1, mahat, which we know is the pause between the expansion and compression phases of an oscillation at a 'point without mass' in the unmanifested energy.

This 'point' will obviously be 'without distinguishing mark,' because it is a point in prakriti, the unmanifested energy, which puts it in the same category as purusha. SVB tells us that all the interactions on the diagram are referenced to mahat, and from that I understand mahat and buddhi are entangled, which would mean that any discrimination made by buddhi on any other evolute is always compared against the information available at mahat.

Srinivasan has said in Sankhya Karika that any interaction on the diagram must derive from the first interaction, *which, axiomatically, will be an interaction between mahat and the evolute being considered by buddhi.* SVB says much the same when he said that all interactions are referenced against mahat. Considering the diagram as a full process, the context within the subject being measured by buddhi, would be present across the whole diagram.

Earlier, I quoted from SVB, *'The figure unfolds from Prakriti at the top into a descending series of evolutes, each of which submerge into the immediately preceding cause from which it emerged; finally, all phenomena dissolve into prakriti. The cycles of creations and dissolutions, because of the inherent nature of prakriti, are endless ...*

If, as Patanjali and SVB tell me, this diagram represents an endless process, then the process follows on from the initial moment of apprehension, step by retained step, because reality holds the retained information of past, present, and future; and at the end of the retained outcome, it has returned to its starting context of that moment, because it is endless. This can be achieved because every step is compared against mahat, making each conscious moment of buddhi a quantum measurement on mahat, which yields the appropriate next step in that process.

This is the process, and irrespective of whether the subject itself is sentient or inorganic, it can produce mind, memory, and matter. For example, the only context operating in the moment of singularity is the context present at the beginning of the next step in the cycle, which initiates the steps to create the manifestative cause (MC^2) of a photon, described in Genesis as 'let there be light.'

This would account for the simultaneous harmonics within that fundamental waveform, which have different qualities or interactions at each of the different points/evolutes on the diagram. This has solved another contradiction relating to mahat, which was that this space is the same space in which Prakriti, the unmanifest energy, is reflected upon by Purusha.

At the bottom of the diagram, we find the gross elements, which are the fields and forces of the fundamental process of creating, sustaining, and dissolution within the cyclic model of Sankhya's philosophy and physics. I am not saying this is how physicists see it, but from outside of physics, it is how it is from my perspective.

The gross elements represent everything needed at the point in a process employing a series of moments as the context in which the first matter is created and is also the process of the 'nothing' at the end of a cycle, which employs the same gross elements in the series of moments as the context running the process in reverse to create wholeness-in-a-black-hole. This gave me the clues to be able to link the diagram to GS's Sankhya and his version of the physics within this 'descent of consciousness into matter.'

The commentary given for the diagram is primarily focused from that perspective, and what I needed to provide was Srinivasan's alternative view of the diagram to bring it in line with what Bohm sought to support his concept of wholeness and the implicate order. I think the four words, earth, water, fire, and air, at the bottom of the diagram can represent the forces of gravity, electro/magnetism, the strong nuclear force, and the weak nuclear force. The fifth word, space, which SVB applies to Akasha, the greatest teacher, but it can now be seen to be the quantum information related to the other four words, and collectively these five 'gross elements' are described by Srinivasan in his translation of Sankhya Karika[5], and I have described how it works from that perspective in chapter 4, and I reiterate here to refresh the reader's mind.

GS defines what I think is the equilibrium and disequilibrium of prakriti, as a harmonic oscillation which is *coherent, perpetual, dynamic, and unmanifest.* Here, the reader can imagine the waveform of the oscillation being the point which is a singularity or a point without mass, as that of a spherical or cubic standing wave. And since this point is nonlocal and time-asymmetric, every iteration of the harmonics of the fundamental waveform can be capable of interfering with itself within that point. The unmanifest nature of the energy oscillating within the singularity comes from GS's assertion that space is not empty but comes from the fact that all matter resolves back into the unmanifest state at the end of a black hole, which relates directly back to the cyclic nature of prakriti across the whole cosmos. This leaves physical space as a continuum of singularities, each holding the quantum information relative in spacetime to the information of the earlier conscious experiences of mind and matter kept as quantum potentials in a continuum that Bohm called his implicate order. From my perspective outside of physics, Bohm's implicate order can be understood as MC^2, underlying the revolving door of the cosmos that we may call reality, or 'the will of God'.

In his translation of the Sankhya Karika, GS describes the various harmonics within this fundamental spherical standing waveform as being:

1. compressive, tamas, which finally manifests as gravity,
2. sattvic, expansive which becomes consciousness and luminous/ radiative, and
3. rajas, the viewpoint, I am-ness, which impels the other two. In the diagram rajas is above the switching arrow while Ahamkara is below the line, and from my perspective, this provides a clue that Rajas is switching between aspects of information as sattva, a quantum potential and tamas as the manifested forces, fields, and matter arising from the 'gross elements.'

He explains that one reason this space, mahat, is special, is that it represents the momentary pause between the end of a compression phase of the oscillation, and the beginning of the next expansion phase. There is a logical reason the diagram is constructed this way; it draws a distinction between mahat and buddhi, which also is written beside mahat at evolute 1.

GS says that any quantum interaction on the diagram can only be between mahat and buddhi, and one other point on the diagram. To understand this, we need first, to realise that as *mahat and buddhi,* the latter being faculty of *discrimination, intelligence, and intellection,* and *the first vehicle of purusha, are entangled* in the final moment at the end of a black hole, (notwithstanding Hawking's information paradox[20]).

Taking these points together, we find that the first vehicle of purusha, buddhi, entangled with mahat, the moment between two phases of the oscillation, enters prakriti with 'no distinguishing mark.' The distinguishing mark enters through asmita and ahamkara as described earlier.

Now, I go back to Krishnamurti's comment that 'the observer is the observed,' and suggest that buddhi is observing or entangled with every part of the diagram simultaneously as well as selectively moment by moment brought about by quantum asymmetry. So, as GS explained about the quantum interactions which I have applied to the yoga diagram, the first interaction *'which can axiomatically be only between the first two objects,'* must be between buddhi and the momentary pause between the end of one phase of the fundamental oscillation and the beginning the next phase.

There might be no opportunity for any activity at all, but there is another factor to consider. Rajas is impelling sattva and tamas (remember, these two meets to become ego at ahamkara) which really tells us that it is the fundamental oscillations within prakriti's unmanifested energy at mahat buddhi, which impels or switches between the mind, the subjective inputs from the senses, and the objective forces produced by the corresponding gross elements, through which buddhi compares the momentary collective memory from the perspective of ego, non-self (ahamkara), against the memory of universal self.

I note here that when I use the word, memory, I include the context of an experience as well as its subjective and objective components. From my perspective, it is quite likely that buddhi's discrimination was deduced by some of the ancients to be a conscious judgement, hence the almost universal belief in a judgemental god. To be objectively honest, it is our own humanity present in asmita/ego that judges every moment in time in the human mind.

This consciousness of sattva in action, is buddhi at evolute1, mind (objective) at evolutes 3-13, and tamas (subjective) at evolutes 14-23. If buddhi is entangled with tamas, then the activity which produced the pain, joy, and experience physically, is entangled (known) at buddhi as mind and body, and we become conscious of it. It also modifies the mind, which provides a 'distinguishing mark' or identity for the information of that moment in that universal self, and we call that modification a memory.

I use the term, 'fundamental oscillation,' because it is the same process as I used to describe mind and memory. The only difference is the context; in the case of the moment at the end of a black hole, the most recent information retained is the context of knowing that all the former matter has become 'pure' unmanifested energy, which, when it is discriminated by buddhi, becomes the context for the preparation of a process to create the manifestative cause necessary to manifest the neutrons, electrons, fields, and forces, which create a photon, and, eventually, the local gravity to hold things together for hydrogen to form, then the next form of matter on the periodic table, and on it goes ...

Therefore, from my understanding at least, the singularities that exist in every point throughout conventional space, are the underlying principle of Bohm's wholeness. I recognise the fact that I have not accounted for his certainty, and we will get to that soon enough, but first, we have a bit more to say about the diagram. There is more to say about why I think differently, and what that difference might be in terms of the yoga diagrams.

The 23 evolutes, of which the universe is constituted, and which form out personalities, are all non-self. The intelligence and faculty of discrimination, through ego and mind and all their attendant cognitions, volitions, emotions, inclinations, all the physical senses as well as what they sense, their components as well as the states of the physical body too, they are all non-self. Only the spiritual-energy principle is the self. This realisation alone eradicates all pain permanently and totally.

This alone is final freedom; at least it can be freedom for the serious and resolute student of Patanjali's yoga sutras. For the rest of us, it is the self-induced cycle of repetition of the past, a past from which the people who brought the Vedas from the Arctic Circle were safely isolated for a time. Then came a recognition of the changing nature of their climate. There were fewer humans in that period estimated to be around 30,000 years ago as mentioned in Tilak's book, *The Arctic Home in the Vedas*[13]. I don't really know when they reached Asia Minor, where they dispersed, but their influence is evident in the cultures of the regions they passed on their journey. From what I read in that book, they passed through China, as well as Persia, with others travelling northward into Northern Europe according to Tilak, before finally settling in the Indus Valley, in 10,000-15,000BC.

This journey was recorded in the Vedas and formed the basis for the Bhagavad-Gita, Mahabharata, Upanishads, yoga sutras, and others. Having a more permanent home, these people became acquainted with their neighbours and shared their knowledge with travellers and traders. I can only guess that their neighbours would be interested in their beliefs because in the Indus Valley region there are a number of similar religions that have been recorded from a time before Alexander the Great went to India.

The Vedic people shared their knowledge of science, philosophy, medicine, chemistry, and mathematics with the Greeks, who subsequently brought some of that knowledge to Egypt and from there to Moses. Most of the Western civilisations gained parts of that Vedic knowledge which became incorporated into their beliefs and practices, but the source was later acknowledged as Greek and Roman over time.

In a separate book from 1880, *Paradise Found: The Cradle of the Human Race at the North Pole*,[14] by William Warren. This book of comparative religions supposes all religions have evolved from these people who left the Arctic Circle, and this book's researcher has a similar account to that developed by Tilak[10].

The Greek version of this knowledge lacked the composite knowledge of the Vedas, and Bohm's dilemma is the result of that missing knowledge. Through a twist of irony, similar to the dual nature of the Vedas, and later of the yoga sutras, that duality was revealed when the Australian theological historian, Dr Barbara Thiering, wrote her translation of those ancient texts in the Dead Sea Scrolls, covering the period when Judea, a protectorate under the Roman Empire, was governed by the Jewish king, Herod.

Thiering's translation sets the scene for the transition from a Jewish sect known as the Essenes, which became Christianity. Jesus was a member of that sect, and Dr Thiering covers the life of Jesus in these books, quoted herein. *Jesus the Man*[15], and *The Book that Jesus wrote*[16].

What was of interest to me was the method used to include different interpretations of the text. Dr Thiering uses the Hebrew name of the method as a 'Pesher,' a concealed duality, similar the duality inferred above. I recognised the pesher as a same or similar method as used in the Vedas for concealing the Sankhya science embedded in the spiritual text of Patanjali's yoga sutras, described by GS in his translation of the Sankhya sutras to obtain their scientific context.

I am not about to incorporate Dr Thiering's books in this book, only to observe that the political machinations of the various sects, political parties, opposition parties, royal houses, and districts, are no different from the Machiavellian practises found today in every level of government, be that local, national, or international. What is concerning me is that her work has shown me that we humans still adhere to much of the perpetuated form of planned ignorance as the means to every end.

This is why, in the preface, I suggested this book may find its use as a productive format through which we might explore an understanding of thinking and consciousness, and with that understanding, we might fashion a more effective model for human relationships to benefit all forms of life in a local, national, or international context. I would welcome seeking a fresh understanding of consciousness in relationships of the personal and universal variety, and any steps in that direction will be an alternative to the universal cost, human and financial, which is embedded in the current model of human intercourse.

I am tempted to think that we are doing what the yoga diagram has shown to be the human condition, because it is the same human condition described in the *Dead Sea Scrolls*; a sharp contrast to what we have in the Vedas, Sankhya, and the yoga sutras. Yes, at the cosmological level, life creation is cyclic, but as the Vedic people have shown in their Vedas, there have been situations in the past in which people have lived successfully together without violence in a journey, which must have covered a millennium or more to reach their end point, which was half the world away from their starting point.

It is so easy for us humans to assume that our brains are superior to other species, and we offer the observation of our lives and languages to justify that assumption. But the other species suffer trauma, respond to love and danger, and even plan strategies for coping with present and future dangers based on past experiences. What I learned from my experience with the cat is that every form of life has its own specie-specific mc^2 or manifestative cause operating through its own specie-specific sensory and response system, or shall I just call it the same senses and subtle and gross elements.

I do not have any magic potion or method, and in the current mental human construct, even if one were available, many people would interpret it as operating against their personal warped/ imagined understanding of what the word freedom means. On the yoga diagram, that notion of freedom is based on ego, I-am-ness, which is the only form of equality we have; *'I am your equal, but cannot be too sure about you, until you prove you are equal to me, by my standards.'*

In a more equitable model, I would look for something like, 'I can only offer the thoughts I know well enough to explain them, and I have no desire to make my thoughts the callipers for measuring your own thoughts.'

The answer may be that we can start by having a practical model of consciousness which incorporates the various levels of consciousness that exists without the recognition of physics and philosophy, but we can only begin if we have the determination to replace the existing enigmas with valid proof. That validation will only come about if we can agree the current theory of mind must be set aside and accept there are diverse levels of consciousness, one more subjective that the other, and neither is superior to the other. This is because we are all in a state of transition, and instead of our present categorising of people in terms of 'illness' we might try finding productive ways to assist their transition to the next level.

There is no reason to discard our systems of belief when there is sufficient evidence that they all reflect the same desire for peace and harmony within a common set of parameters. For example, all insist there is only one God, and yet we know that all cultures have a different name for that one universal God. If we give up on the issue of whether identity is an existential determinant and instead can accept the physical fact of MC^2 which really operates on matter, living or inorganic, then we must step off the treadmill of inter-denominational warfare. How can it be cool to believe there is only one God, and at the same time be prepared to kill someone because their God has a different name. Who gave God a name anyway? And how can that be necessary when there is agreement on there being only one God with different names?

If that agreement is accepted, we can stop the conflict and approach the enigma of mind and consciousness with an open mind. In chapter 3 of the yoga sutras of Patanjali I was intrigued by YS.1.17, in which we find: *'The sound, the message within the sound, and the idea behind the message, all exist within the sound. By meditating in the Samadhi state all three can be clearly understood.'*

A common starting point for us could be found in a relatively-recent position, beginning with Moses Maimonides from only 800-900 years ago, and as a reference, we could use his book, *"A Guide for the Perplexed,*[17]*"* in which Maimonides made an important point which, in the context of the Yoga sutras, is strikingly relevant here when he said, *"God has no attributes."*

I find his observation synonymous with Patanjali's phrase *'without distinguishing mark,'* but equally obscure in a context of physics and philosophy. When I consider his phrase as a pesher, I find his observation that God has no attributes to be an obvious connection to the yoga sutras and the Vedas.

This is where the notion of defining humans as 'chosen by God' can only be valid if it applies to all humans, and it becomes even more questionable when we define humans as being 'made in God's image.' If we are all made in God's image I fail to understand why there is an almost universal acceptance of the notion that God is male.

At conception, the embryo begins as female and for some reason that is conveniently ignored. Do we really mean that women are not created in God's image? This idea of God needs to be challenged or redefined as neuter in terms of gender.

I found the advice that *to 'define is to limit,'* attributed to Oscar Wilde[10] is why there is such a problem when we use the word, freedom. The limit currently in use comes into play with the notion, *'It's my way or the highway,'* as the individual definition of freedom. If all humans are equal, this can only be true if we apply that same freedom to everyone. There cannot ever be any individual freedom in a community without an agreed set of constraints to maintain personal health and safety through an agreed set of rules we call LAW. The only circumstance in which there is individual freedom is that freedom available to an individual monk or nun alone in his/her cell meditating in the Samadhi state.

It is obvious that we humans continue to use our inherited simian traits when it comes to learning, which we do by imitating or copying the obviously beneficial acts of others, such as the reported observation of 'the hundredth monkey' washing its fruit or vegetable before eating it.

Earlier, I related Einstein's MC^2 to 'manifestative cause,' mentioned in the yoga sutras. Now I am inviting the reader to revise that manifestative cause to be atman which, like MC^2, cannot have a valid distinguishing mark if it is defining the universal self. In its place there is only the individual ego, I-am-ness, in which we define ourselves by our specific aggregates of subtle and gross elements within our own level of consciousness.

These gross elements manifest as conscious opportunities or risks, accompanied by subconscious options, which, in a general situation, can take around 200 or more milliseconds to reach our conscious mind as a decision or answer to a question. This is why philosophers require the subjective component of consciousness to be present in a theory of mind, and unfortunately, what happens during those milliseconds is the enigma because it is a sum over histories calculation made by purusha's conscious quantum potential, buddhi. In a situation involving other people it may take longer, depending on the state of our ego in terms of others, a cost/benefit question.

Knowledge of this different level of consciousness will remain outside of that theory of mind, not because it is an enigma; it is because at that different level of consciousness there are axioms based on the memory of genuine experience rather than opinions in what may be a theory of everyone and everything.

In my earlier book, *"Thinking on the Other Side of Zero,"* the foreword was written by my mentor, Dr Bevan Reid, and he said that to think like Oliver one would have to employ the imaginary number *i*, and I have given a lot of thought about what he could mean because *i*, the square root of -1.

When I think of that imaginary number from my weird perspective, the -1 represents the entanglement of a real number, 1, and an unmanifested number 1, which must be a form of asymmetric polarity. Who knows? It may simply be a form of mathematics, about which I know nothing.

I can only think of using this imaginary number, *i*, is there to remind us that these quantum interactions on the yoga diagram result from an observation by the consciousness of Purusha in the superconscious state.

I am sure my mention of the superconscious state will get the reader's attention, but I haven't used that term as a hook. I have thought about *i*, for some time, and when I think of the yoga diagram as the unmanifested energy Patanjali asserts to be, then is becomes obvious that anyone trying to understand the diagram must keep this in mind.

The superconscious state is a higher level of consciousness that I have been unaware of for most of my life, and it is the reason I have struggled to understand myself, and why my interactions with everyone can be difficult at times.

There is no offence intended in what I have written; this book has only ever been about introducing the reader to think differently, and even if only one sentence has done that for just a little while, it can provide the chance to question the ideas we hold dearly. What is here for the taking is the transition, atha, which may be a welcome relief or a challenge. I only ask that you, the reader, take responsibility for your response and congratulate yourself for any difference it has, or has not made, in terms of what you *can think*.

I am aware that you as the reader may disagree with what I have written, but please realise that any agreement or disagreement is the product of you thinking consciously to reach your decision to agree or disagree. This gives you the option of looking back on the yoga diagram and tracking the path you have taken in this previously unconscious process. Now that I have written in a general sense what I have learned from the yoga sutras, and Sankhya, I must address the enigma itself because it is not as great a challenge as one might think.

Yoga diagram

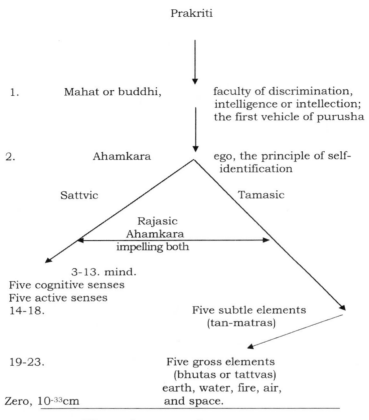

Prakriti

1.   Mahat or buddhi,   faculty of discrimination,
                                          intelligence or intellection;
                                          the first vehicle of purusha

2.   Ahamkara   ego, the principle of self-
                                              identification

        Sattvic   Tamasic

                    Rajasic
                    Ahamkara
                 impelling both

             3-13. mind.
        Five cognitive senses
        Five active senses
        14-18.   Five subtle elements
                                              (tan-matras)

        19-23.   Five gross elements
                                          (bhutas or tattvas)
                                          earth, water, fire, air,
        Zero, 10⁻³³cm   and space.

Physical space and atomic matter
Fig.6.1.

I have added a line below evolutes 19-23, to indicate a notional
quantum interface between the unmanifested energy at the
final evolute where matter becomes atomic, and the space where
information is retained. Everything above the line describes the
reflection of Purusha's consciousness (Sattva), as it selectively knows
every potential of the Bohm's potential (the subtle elements) which
become active to manifest the whole reality.

The other five gross elements consist of the potentials for the four fundamental (real) forces of physics retained in Akasha, which is the 'space' below the line which 'retains' information that subsequently manifests as mind and physical matter.

From that perspective, I can say that evolutes 14-18, and 19-23, make up Patanjali's manifestative cause in YS.1.11., which I say is Einstein's MC^2, to produces the fundamental forces, locality, spacetime, and the information within Bohm's Implicate Order, all of which are information as quantum potentials.

Two less obvious points regarding manifestative cause are the potential giving rise to reincarnation of an individual, and the less obvious manifestative cause arising from past generations in a person's DNA, mentioned in religions as sins being passed to following four or more generations.

From quantum mechanics, we know that in the virtual or quantum state, time is asymmetric, and since time is a mental concept, it will have some relationship to consciousness, which means that every observation made by Purusha is retained in the virtual space of Akasha. In my view, every quantum interaction on the diagram will be retained in Akasha, which infers that every quantum interaction on the diagram is asymmetric in the spacetime of mind.

Applying this last point to every observation by purusha, I can also infer that consciousness itself is asymmetric, as would be every singularity, spacetime, non-locality and locality, are all asymmetric. Considering every singularity point throughout the whole cosmos, I can say the continuous conscious observations made by Purusha in the virtual/quantum state can be the basis for understanding Purusha's (God's) omniscience, omnipotence, and omnipresence.

Since all religions have this common belief, it should be possible to have religion and science agree on this point as an axiom rather than a belief based on faith. Using the diagram, we can all understand that God and/or Purusha 'knows' everything that can be known, because every observation, past, present, and future, exists in that virtual state. Moreover, in that virtual state there is no separation between cause and effect for the same time-asymmetric reason given above. Thus, I can say that Einstein's MC^2, as Patanjali's manifestative cause, is also asymmetric.

What can be less obvious is that every observation is a conscious observation because Purusha/God is conscious. What is more difficult to understand is that the communication with God/Purusha is through the Samadhi state; it is the coalescence of two minds, and this means that we 'know' and the information manifests through our senses, meaning we know through which sense is dominant in the individual. Some 'see' God, others 'feel' God's presence, while others can 'hear' God's voice. These perceptions of communication are what Patanjali described as 'manifestative cause.' Thus, a male 'priest' will hear a 'male' God while a priestess will hear a female God.

The selection of these 'aspects' of God are inherent in all living forms, but the manifestative cause also manifests in non-living matter. Patanjali tells us that *when there is a conjunction of a number of points without mass, a point with mass can appear.* Here the manifestative cause is still the basic collection of the necessary parameters, and these are the relationship between Purusha's/God's observation and its context in a moment and location of that observation. When the fundamental forces and conditions align, a particle of hydrogen, or a photon, can appear 'out of nothing.' The same is true of the cyclic nature of manifestation. Yoga tells us that the cycle consists of (1). creation, (2). sustaining, and (3). dissolution.

I have been asked what happens when we die, and in terms of the yoga diagram it is obvious that the five subtle elements and the five gross elements are withdrawn in a process that reflects the absence of these ten components together or part by part, based on the physical circumstances arising from the accrued karma of the individual. From my own experience, after the individual dies there can be the experience of intense bliss.

In answering the question of how long a person remains in between the actual death and moving on, I am confident that this is only related to the manifestative cause, which means how long the living tissue remains alive after the technical 'death.' I guess some parts may remain in a 'living state' for the time cells have sufficient oxygen to be 'alive,' but it is a pointless question, because there is no avenue for any responses from the brain to maintain 'life' as we know it.

Psychic friends have referred to my recovery from a near death experience as one in which this current Alan was a 'walk in,' because in this incarnation the incoming soul (or consciousness) has avoided the trauma of birth. This raises a few thoughts about my body having its original DNA, and my mind having a different manifestative cause brought in by my current soul.

As for the 'soul' itself, that is always a part of the individual 'manifestative cause,' and will enter into another conception with its own karmic 'baggage.' The question of how long the soul waits between incarnations is irrelevant because the soul is in the time asymmetric state between incarnations, and there is no time as well as all time in that state.

What is of interest is the concept of space as a continuum of singularities because it is in these singularities that the manifestative cause operates. You, the individual, are spread across all the space ever occupied by your body, and you move from that collection of singularities to the next. Your momentary experience is active in that individual space and precedes your body as you move through real space.

The same is true of the sun and the planets, with their fixed orbits. Each follows Patanjali's cyclic model of dissolving and reforming in another adjacent point moment by moment. Light is a physical phenomenon, and the light from the sun or a star, travels in that same manner, from manifesting in one point, absorbed in the closest point and radiates from that point to every other point. From the perspective of the observer, the light travels in a straight line to the observer, human, or measuring device. This is the time we measure to calculate the speed of light. On the other hand, the quantum interactions of information on the yoga diagram would be spacetime asymmetric and appear to travel 'faster than the speed of light.'

So, we do have enough knowledge to resolve any chasm between religion and science if we want to do that. There will be times when the absence of objectivity is the reason we find the resolution of the most fundamental questions are out of reach. Finding an answer for a theory of consciousness is one of those absences. The objectivity needed is hidden by the insistence of philosophers that an explanation for the subjective component is necessary for such a theory to be valid.

I have been caught in a similar dilemma for most of my life, where the absence of the subjective component in my thinking process makes any idea I have being dismissed out of hand. What Patanjali's yoga sutras have shown me is that these two conflicting components reflect the whole reality we all seek to understand, in which each is necessary if we are serious about understanding reality from Bohm's perspective of wholeness.

I have a few points unanswered, beginning with Bohm's certainty that an answer would come from outside of physics. He was right, especially in terms of wholeness because the idea, outside of physics, exists simultaneously with physics *in the undivided whole.*

His certainty comes from the incomplete answer to his question that already existed in the manifestative cause of his question at 'space' on the yoga diagram. And like so much in the discipline we call education, definitions rule, and answers such as the one regarding his certainty remain unanswered because he had not asked the right question. The absence of the right question applies in the answer to the question of why I think differently. Bohm was correct when he said the answer to his question about wholeness would come from outside of physics, and he had obviously thought about wholeness from the perspective of physics and had concluded that physics was incomplete in that respect.

There is a natural tendency to only believe what we can measure, and in my case this applies to the 'non-scientific' answers regarding a Near-Death-Experience, which involve the person having that experience and describing it as an experience of being 'out of my body.'

What I was able to learn from Emma was that what was 'out of her body' was the conscious observer; in her case the conscious observer was the midwife at Emma's own birth. That example takes our conversation back to the enigma of Samapatti, and its relevance to conscious memory through Patanjali's 'manifestative cause.' In every Samapatti, there is the seer, where the individual seer becomes conscious of the subject's manifestative cause, and therefore, has the subject's subjective experience. As Krishnamurti said, the observer is the observed. It would have helped had he followed with 'and vice versa,' because both are conscious through buddhi, whose consciousness is that of purusha.

We need to understand that all consciousness is that of purusha, the seer, and we all are the subject who is separate in a physical sense, and, simultaneously, conscious in the sense of the universal soul, atman. This may sound complicated, but to understand consciousness and wholeness, we must go back to the asymmetry in the Samadhi state.

It is fine to acknowledge time asymmetry, but in that state, everything is asymmetric, including consciousness. The obvious example is location, which science calls nonlocality. I am inclined to say that in the Samadhi state there is location asymmetry, and I can live with nonlocality because it indicates that physicists understood that particular asymmetry. I guess the term, 'zero-point energy,' comes from that same asymmetry in the unmanifested energy at the final moment of a black hole.

Memory is the product of time asymmetry in that every conscious interaction is ever-present, giving the impression that the interaction is 'retained' or 'recorded,' when, in fact, every conscious interaction is simultaneous, and can only become personal as a conscious memory. Bohm's sense of wholeness is due to the fact that *there is only one self which is knowing the interaction,* and can discriminate between it and the previous interaction, which means we can say that consciousness arises from the fact of *self-asymmetry.*

For the individual, this means there are always two strands of consciousness: *purusha,* the real self, and non-self, *ahamkara.* All individuals identify with the latter and rationalise between the two, if, and when, they are aware of these two streams. We are limited by the belief that it is our body which is conscious, and we can 'prove' that belief by the evidence we get from measuring stimuli and responses in the brain.

To end on a historical note, Maimonides, back in 1160's, writing to one of his students, had decided to call his book *A Guide for the Perplexed*, because he had found that in trying to understand the prophets' words, people try to rationalise those words into 'today-speak,' rather than let the words lead the mind to 'God's will', which can only be accessible in the Samadhi state. Of course, he didn't use the word Samadhi; I have tried to deduce his meaning because it is pertinent to the words of SVB and GS.

'There is only one God' is an axiom and as such has no need for a distinguishing mark, and I understand that to mean God has no human name because history shows that whenever mankind gives God a name, which can infer exclusivity on a part of the whole of mankind, there is always disagreement on the name of God if it differs from the name others have already given their God.

For millennia humankind has built a no-go zone between religion and science, and to some extent that boundary also exists between religion and philosophy. What GS shows in his translation of Sankhya is that the boundary is unnecessary for those who can think the way Patanjali thought, because the yoga sutras embody both perspectives which, with some honest non-partisan thought, can be understood from both perspectives.

We can begin with an honest appraisal of $E = MC^2$, and have a conversation about manifested and unmanifested states, and about space as a continuum of singularities. It does not take much effort to think of each of those infinite singularities as a quantum of local information; Déjà vu is a good example of what has been known in the history related to a location; just think of battle sites as an example where many people today can experience the pain of earlier humans involved in those events.

My attempts to explain the momentary interactions of information as potentials can be extrapolated to a simple model in which each quantum moment represents the moment-by-moment manifestation and dissolution of a real particle as it, as part of a whole planet, moves through the cosmos by dissolving at one point and manifesting at an adjacent point in step with every other particle of that planet, resulting in the whole planet moving on a known trajectory.

On the one hand, some would say this is the explanation of the physics of a galaxy; on the other hand, it is an explanation of how God manages this whole reality. Does it really matter if we use 'manifestative cause' or 'God's will' in the explanation?

I am sure a planet or galaxy does not ask those questions and yet the cosmos continues to manifest galaxies in which planets and galaxies collapse into black holes without any fuss at all.

CHAPTER 7

Bohm's Wholeness and the Implicate Order

David Bohm's implicate order is a fact of reality across the whole cosmos, evident in every living species. The invariable nature of this order is absent in the Homo Sapiens form because of our delusion in the way we think. Our forebears were able to find ways to exploit the natural order around them to accommodate their evolution from their simian cousins. It was a necessary change in their adaptation from life in the forest to life on the savannah and its predators. We adapted in some ways but retained the structures of family and grouping for a more effective model of survival.

As I look at Bohm's implicate order, and the model described in the yoga sutras, it clear to me that nature has always had an inherent rules-based order which was known by our early deep-thinkers, and this order was respected in every culture as the over-arching being or creator. Through millennia this led to systems of thought, which incorporated that central belief into what we now know as 'God's will' in all religions.

In terms of time, we have the great trekking 'out of Africa,' over millennia, giving rise to the different Homo species in various parts of the world in various times. The humans who entered the Arctic Circle in a temperate period were subjected to cycles of six months of darkness and six months of daylight, a situation which fostered observation of nature and the night sky, and the subsequent questioning of their observations. When their observations revealed the onset of glaciation, this culture migrated to warmer climes in the south, ending in the Indus Valley, Persia, and the Germanic regions.

Another isolated group from Africa had moved through the South Pacific and were able to walk or canoe into what is now Australia because of the lower sea levels, resulting from the glaciation of the polar regions. Like their northern human cousins, they too became close observers of their environment and food sources, developing similar rules-based systems about their relationship with the country.

A later migration out of Africa were the modern humans who settled in the Middle East and European regions, a migration which is continuing even now with refugees from every part of the planet as they seek to escape poverty and conflict in which they have been caught up by other cultures' rules-based order.

Every day we can see on the news where interpretations of the original rules-based order are exploited for personal gain in the many forms of capitalism, communism, socialism, and democracy, and we ask ourselves, why?

The answer to our question is there on yoga diagram at evolute 2, (Ahamkara, ego, I am), while the only rules-based system capable of managing our problem, buddhi, is at evolute 1. Yoga tells us that reality is cyclic, and that buddhi, implicit at the quantum level, has its own faculty of discrimination which operates independently of our systems of belief and governance.

Of the four forms of rules-based order listed above, democracy is the closest form of order capable of providing an equal share of benefit and safety for everyone everywhere, but *only when ego is set aside for the greater good*. This equality for everyone everywhere is the measure we can only assume to be in place as 'God's will.' The notion of 'God's will' is the basis for a 'loving and just but judgemental God,' but in fact, it goes far deeper than that.

As a quantum information entity, buddhi is a permanent fixture in the model of reality, discriminating every moment of every singularity's 'sum over histories' to create the context of the next moment for that singularity, and without any change in the way we think, we will always have cycles of systems of belief and governance. In short, we as individuals must set aside the current infatuation with personal identity and ideas of separateness from every other individual. There is only *one* self, in many bodies and in many species; nobody can be separate from everybody, despite of what one might think. Separateness is the grand delusion, and we need to get over it. To do that, everyone must set aside personal gain and identity for everyone's benefit.

I can remember watching a video of a conversation between David Bohm and Krishnamurti in the mid-80s; it was about the state of the world at the time, and they quoted a statement which, if I remember correctly, came from Einstein. The statement was: *The state of the world in any moment in time will always be the direct consequence of the way we think, and we cannot make any correction state of the world by thinking in this present way; we must find a better way of thinking.*

That video conversation left its impression on me, and there is a constant connection to theirs or Einstein's challenge which is reiterated in mind every time I read a newspaper or watch a news broadcast at any time of a day, week, month, or year. There is an incessant torrent of calamity, crime, war, climate predictions and accusations and every form of chaos imaginable. As I write this I notice that all of the manufactured chaos infers a causal link between every one of the momentary dramas as a validation of Bohm's wholeness. What I see is the relevance between this chaos and the point Einstein made about the need to think in an entirely unusual way.

In what I have written so far, I have used the different perspectives I experienced in the Samadhi state of Samapatti to draw attention to the incomplete theory of mind and the hard problem of consciousness and other points made in the book. I will try to put forward the salient points I have found from the yoga sutras, the Sankhya, and my experiences as a private researcher. Now, I will attempt to find some yogi sense amid all this existential noise.

Einstein has pointed out the problem is related to the way the world thinks, *meaning the way everyone thinks;* nobody is left out of this problem, which makes sense because there is only one self. It means I have to find a common cause embedded in all the life forms of the world. That is fairly straightforward because what is common in every species is life; that becomes the starting point, or in quantum terminology it is the starting state of an interaction, indeed every interaction leading to a transition, *atha,* the first word in the first yoga sutra.

In a cyclic universe, creation is about creating matter from unmanifested energy, and first matter is the photon. We can skip that and the whole periodic table because the elements are obviously not to blame for the state of the world today. No, the chaos is an outcome from living forms, which brings evolution into focus.

From the first appearance of life, evolution was primarily about supply and demand of the necessities of life which one could say was initially pre-cellular or single cellular, with a simple form of Maslow's hierarchy of needs; food, warmth, and procreation.

The world today has moved on a little bit and the disorder is emanating from the Homo species who dominate the food chain. Humans are intelligent in manner different from other species in that we use language and have larger brains in terms of body mass, and it is that intelligence which is driving our chaos. I base that opinion on the fact that humans think in a way that differs from the evolved way other species think.

If one looks back at the first simple life form in terms of the yoga diagram, the same fundamental process which produced a practical self-replicating living form is the process we use today; what has changed is the context of self-replicating applies to us because it is based, as always, on memory, location and spacetime. The notable change was the change from replication by cell division to sexual reproduction.

In Ys 1.11, the last part of the description of the sutra describes a different kind of memory in which it is not about the *cognition of an object* which is primary; what is primary is the *process and instrument of apprehension,* which Patanjali tells us is *intelligence* because it is the consciousness of purusha at evolute 1, buddhi, on the yoga diagram.

Earlier I talked about intuition, and we can trace that faculty back to the first appearance of life which would, through buddhi, have that faculty. And since those species reproduced through cell division, each division was a replica of the former cell; all were effectively the same cell in every life form and that remained after the evolution of sexual reproduction in which there is still cell division in that system, and it begins after conception.

We know from science that the ovum produced by a woman is female; a cellular clone of the woman herself, and at conception the sperm will provide the possibility of a male or female embryo, and at some later stage of the pregnancy the embryo can change to a male embryo. What is important to note is that the embryo, initially female, has a direct continuous life line back to the first appearance of life, and therefore, through buddhi has the potentially continuous memory and manifestative causes of this continuous or universal life.

We call this intuition, and it is the equivalent of Maslow's hierarchy of needs based, not on many lifetimes of a woman's experience but on the experience of every life since that first appearance of life because life as a quantum state is retained in the same manner that memory is retained.

Here, I must make it abundantly clear that the retention of experience is retained in the quantum or virtual state, not as some universal data cache, but through the asymmetric state of virtual information which is time asymmetric, location asymmetric and response asymmetric.

The intelligence, mentioned in relation to the *process and instrument of apprehension is intuition* (which we find in the descriptions of memory and Samapatti in Samadhi pada), and is the superconscious state, which is why my memory of an experience is objective rather than subjective. And it is why intuition is also that same superconscious state which presented the context (as a memory) for a living form of matter to manifest from singularity in the unmanifested energy. This is what Bohm was suggesting when he said that an explanation for wholeness would come from 'outside of physics.'

The word intuition infers the teacher within, and Patanjali has called that teacher Mahat/buddhi at the first evolute on the diagram. Patanjali applies that same title to space and from my perspective this means the manifested space (spacetime) and the unmanifested nonlocal space of Bohm's quantum potential. I can confidently assume the consciousness of Purusha (the reflection of which on prakriti is present in Mahat/buddhi), is consciously and selectively entangled across the whole yoga diagram, which means it is the universal observer.

In other words, at that first evolute on the Yoga diagram, this fundamental consciousness/God is 'without distinguishing mark' in the unmanifested energy and is free to be consciously and selectively entangled with every other evolute on the diagram. This aspect of being consciously selectively active across the whole diagram is where the notion of God/Mahat/ buddhi having free will was recognised by yogis in that Siddhi state; today scientists and philosophers might call it superconsciousness.

In my view, superconsciousness is Einstein's other way of thinking; if we need to find a better way of thinking, I will suggest we must think like God if we want to do God's will, which is not as complicated as one may think. Most of the dystopia in human thinking comes from the fact that most of the personal power exercised in the world, e.g., governance, economic, security and financial is based on identity and gender. This is not exclusively a human trait, but in our species it has been exercised more by men than women, and explains why women think differently from men, and little has changed in that respect since our evolution from our simian forebears or the first forms of life.

To even contemplate the question of thinking in an entirely unique way, we must remember that we are all part of the one Self which we call God, and our prayers to God for a resolution of our question are really prayers to us, asking us to do as Einstein asked, by thinking in an entirely unique way. I would say thinking is a process defined by thinking as an individual self rather than a collective or universal self, and for most of us that would require one to voluntarily surrender her/his individual self to the universal Self.

In view of the almost universal definition of identity which infers an indestructible connection between the body and the mind as me, this one individual who I am, this self. This model of self is easily understood and has given the accepted theory of mind and consciousness the imprimatur it enjoys today. This theory is supported by the evidence available from brain scanning and measurements, and from the demonstrated relationships between thoughts, emotions, the sensory stimuli, and responses, none of which being us any closer to the mythical state of superconsciousness. This brings our discussion back to Patanjali's Yoga Sutras and this mysterious process of the cycles of manifestation of energy into matter and back to the unmanifested state.

The final evolutes on the Yoga diagram are known as the subtle elements and the gross elements. This is where energy and information combine to provide Einstein's M with his C^2. From my reading of the Yoga Sutras, the ancient ones who found this information in the Samadhi or Siddhi state had a direct knowledge of the products coming from the numerous entanglements of the quantum potential, knowledge of the activity within his Implicate Order which Bohm had deduced but hadn't defined in terms of physics.

What the diagram tells us is the consciousness in question is dynamic, it exists, and is unmanifested energy as GS explained in his Sankhya Karika. Patanjali's lesson for us all is that what is absent from the theory of mind is the dynamic consciousness, which is Einstein's C^2, and it is a quantum interaction between Mahat/buddhi, and all the other evolutes consciously entangled within the unmanifested space of Prakriti.

Mahat/buddhi participates in the creation of matter as well as information in the form of intelligence. This intelligence is what is experienced objectively by a yogi as an answer to an earlier question as her/his input into this fundamental process. The space in which this process occurs is the continuum of singularities, manifesting in the *not empty* physical space. That information/answer manifests physically for the yogi as real objective experience.

In my Samapatti examples I had the experience of the subject's mind, and therefore I experienced what the subject saw and felt in those moment. Similarly, the subject had the experience of my body and mind's stillness, which is why Samapatti is the coalescence of two minds. Samapatti is a Samadhi/Siddhi state, and after the experience I only ever had the conscious/objective memory of that experience which had been a subjective experience in the moments of that experience was happening. For the subject, not in that objective state, the experience is remembered as a subjective experience, which is why the subject's memory of the experience is a physical and mental memory.

There is no straightforward way to enter this Samadhi/Siddhi state, and any verbal or printed explanation will only produce an imagined memory of what I described verbally or have written herein. Even trying to put into words a description of the nonlocal state and the information interacting as a quantum interaction will be fraught with error because a normal state of mind has no sensory capability for translation a quantum interaction in the nonlocal state.

When I think about Jesus and his miracles I am inclined to think that he had learned to enter that state during his upbringing in the Essene sect. That is the only rational way the 'miracle of Pentecost' can be understood (as Samapatti), and in that state the members of the audience would have heard the speech given by the Apostles (the seer, trained by Jesus), and each member of the audience would hear the words in her/his own language. I say that because I knew that garden in the cat's dream was felt by me as familiar and safe. Similarly, I initially saw the cat's garden from the cat's perspective, and the view changed as soon as I realised I was seeing it from the cat's perspective, a realisation that changed my perspective from the cat's mind to my own.

To summarise my musing on Bohm's Wholeness and the Implicate Order, I will only say that Bohm was right in respect of his proposition that there is an order implicit in the whole reality, as it has been in the past, as it is the present and as it may be in every reality of a theoretical future.

In this book I have shared the experiences I had in my own personal search to understand my mind and the way I think. My search has relied on my memory of the experiences of my Samapatti subjects which gave me the same experiences in those moments in which their minds and mine did indeed coalesce exactly as Patanjali explained in YS 1.11.

What made it possible for me to explain those experiences from my own perspective was the introduction my mentor, the late Bevan Reid MD, gave me into his observations of information in space in his own laboratory experiments. His work corroborated Bohm's work and made it something even I could understand.

What I learned from their work was the distinction between tangible spacetime and virtual spacetime as described in quantum mechanics and, at least from my perspective, as described in the Vedas, in Patanjali's Yoga Sutras and in all religions and philosophies.

I make no claim to being a teacher, but I will use whatever came to mind as I thought of how I might explain this whole reality. There is no structure in what I think; I can only offer the thoughts I had over the past forty years which, in hindsight, are the salient points which, from my perspective, are now relevant in this whole reality and implicit order.

I was able to have experiences in Samapatti which challenged the accepted theory of mind. At one point I was able to speak to the physicist, Basil Hiley after reading the book he had written with David Bohm, "The Undivided Universe." I described my Samapatti experience with the cat, and asked Hiley how would a physicist describe that interaction. He said the only word that he could suggest is 'entanglement.'

That pointed out a need to find what entanglement meant in quantum mechanics, an unknown discipline to me, and I read whatever I could find. That led to physicists, John Wheeler, Richard Feynman, and the term, *sum over histories,* a term Wheeler used to describe Feynman's theoretical quantum interactions.

Sometime later, I was reviewing Patanjali's Yoga Sutra about memory, and the phrase, *manifestative cause,* brought Feynman's *sum over histories* to mind, suggesting to me there can be a connection between Patanjali's spiritual narrative in the sutras and quantum mechanics. It was simply a matter of reading the spiritual narrative from that Quantum mechanics perspective, and it was how my mind understood what I read. In retrospect, I saw it as the same reasoning I employed earlier in this chapter regarding the miracle of Pentecost.

This separate way of reading the Sutras in terms of quantum mechanics had so many spiritual terminologies become more precise, things like creation, omniscience, omnipotent and time asymmetry. Now, I see the word, asymmetry, can apply to consciousness if, and when, I may have to explain the various levels of consciousness available in the normal mind, contrasted to what is available to a mind in the Samadhi state.

This distinction between the normal consciousness identified by the body as self and the asymmetric consciousness in Samadhi/ Siddhi is what I have found so difficult to explain, and then, in a moment while stacking some firewood in the fireplace on preparation for lighting the fire, I noticed an image on the end of a block of firewood and thought it might help in an explanation of information as a potential in the continuum of singularities in space as a potential.

The block of firewood

I noticed the sawn end of one block of firewood had a water or tannin stain. The stain had the form of an image of what to me looked like the outline of a small dog lying down with ears pointing forward. The stain on the other end of the wood block was just a smudge with no suggestion of an image of anything other than a stain on a piece of wood.

As I thought about how an image of a piece of firewood might provide a coherent explanation of quantum information manifesting as physical matter, there are a number of things to take into consideration. In my diagrams in Part 1, I had drawn a line to indicate an interface between the manifested and the unmanifested state. Here in Part 2, I use the word 'entangled' in place of interface to describe the manifested and the unmanifested states as quantum states which can be selectively present in any number of quantum entanglements across the Yoga diagram in a conscious quantum interaction.

What Vyasa's description of Yoga Sutra 1.11., tells me is that:

a. Mahat represents the pause between moments of disequilibrium of the gunas, and is why we can say that Mahat is the default starting condition of every interaction, i.e., buddhi represents the current conscious observation of the entangled evolute(s) selected by buddhi (representing the consciousness of purusha) in that moment.

b. because the observation by buddhi reflects the consciousness of purusha, and that the selection of which evolute is a conscious selection, the outcome of this selection will manifest in the physical state as sensory/mind as a conscious observation, and atomic matter.

c. this is the process that produces the discrimination by buddhi.

Vyasa tells us that asmita is a *composite sentience* which is produced when Mahat/buddhi receives and reflected spirit of purusha plus prakriti sentience, the latter being the mind (evolutes 3-13). This process is twofold; it is the unmanifested quantum information,

111

Mahat/buddhi, which then manifests as sentience (a real sensory knowing we call mind).

If we apply this part of my narrative to the potential for the image on the saw cut surface of the firewood block, the potential for the process which produced the image exists in any living plant as its *manifestative cause* in every cell of the plant, in every moment, conditional on the physical process by which the plant takes in nutrients from its root system and through the leaves. When the plant, a tree in this case, dies, the uptake from the roots ceases and as the wood dries out, the existing water and other chemicals leach throughout the drying wood.

The image we see, regardless of whether the shape of the stain present at the position of the saw-cut is one which a human may liken it to a living form, or any random shape if the location of the saw cut was on a different point along the tree trunk. We tend to see what we want to see, and in a general sense what we 'recognise' comes from our imagination or memory. Indeed, the word, recognise, means 'to know again,' or, as Vyasa explains in YS.1.11., we 'remember' the image as like, or similar to, another memory.

I have used the potential for a common staining substance in the firewood to represent a quantum potential which later presents as a random shape at the point where the wood has been cut with a saw. We can use the saw cut to represent the quantum interface between Buddhi's observation at Mahat on the diagram, manifesting in the mind as "I see this shape of a little dog."

In my concept of Einstein's MC^2 as yoga's *manifestative cause* and Wheeler's *sum over histories*, the manifestative cause is what Patanjali calls a samskara, and the active aspect of that samskara as a potential of quantum information, is known as karma. From my perspective, karma is the individual's total experience in his/her incarnations, and through DNA the karma of generations before her/him. The yoga principle of 'manifestative cause' operating through the consciousness of Purusha/Ishvara, in my view resolves the question of Einstein's relativity in the context of consciousness.

In the case of the firewood block, the potential for the manifestative cause now represents the information related to the chemistry within the now dead tree being accessible to a living observer, we could say is part of the tree's karma. While the observer can be any individual looking at the saw cut, this photo of the saw cut, can be explained as a dispassionate observer's buddhi, which is the process and instrument of apprehension of the universal buddhi, which is the reflected consciousness of purusha.

I remind the reader that the Yoga's model of creation is cyclic, and if we apply that cyclic model to galaxies, or sun-based systems, we find it in the birth of a star and subsequent collapse of the star's system into a black hole. What this cycle of manifestation of matter from 'nothing' (the quantum potential as the final evolutes, subtle and gross elements of earth, air fire, water, and space, all of which become atomic), and the 'unmanifesting' of matter and spacetime at the end of a cycle, this matter and spacetime collapses into a black hole to become 'nothing.' But remember, this 'nothing' is a quantum potential of matter, spacetime and conscious experience.

Observing all of this is the reflection of purusha, meaning the whole cosmic cycle is 'known,' and this 'knowing' is asymmetric consciousness or superconsciousness. The closest science has come to knowing in terms of consciousness is AI, Artificial intelligence, which requires a human to write its software, will obviously limit what is possible for that AI software program to achieve in practice. This is because the AI programmer writing his/her code is using composite sentience, which includes her/his sum over histories; it

113

is not the reflection of purusha, and therefore, will never include superconsciousness.

When we consider the matter in the block of wood as quantum potential we can also think of all the space occupied by every particle of the wood as an individual space/singularity. On the other hand, the space occupied by the programmer holds his/her life experience and expertise; it is also the space in which the program is written by the programmer, and that space will include the local parameters of the organisation and its expectation which employs that programmer.

In the laboratory in which Bevan Reid was researching 'information in space,' he explored the influence of a 10kg piece of lead in the same laboratory space on cell cultures (mouse fibroblasts) which he subjected to the presence of the lead. I am sure the reader can remember the reference to the Ennis article from NewScientist, which was also about retained information.

I mention retained information-in-space again because it is important that we have that firmly in mind in reference to consciousness being in that retained information space, which is also the same space Patanjali called Akasha, my point being that, consciousness, like Akasha, is not a product or process of the body.

CHAPTER 8

Bohm' whole reality as an intelligent system

I begin this chapter by returning to David Bohm's "Wholeness and the Implicate Order," and Swami Rama's Yoga diagram.

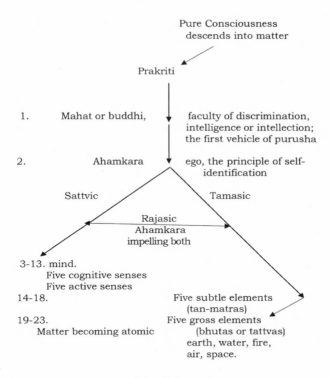

Pure Consciousness
descends into matter

Prakriti

1.   Mahat or buddhi,   faculty of discrimination, intelligence or intellection; the first vehicle of purusha

2.   Ahamkara   ego, the principle of self-identification

Sattvic   Tamasic

Rajasic
Ahamkara
impelling both

3-13. mind.
Five cognitive senses
Five active senses
14-18.   Five subtle elements (tan-matras)
19-23.   Five gross elements
Matter becoming atomic   (bhutas or tattvas) earth, water, fire, air, space.

Fig.8.1.

The whole Yoga diagram is a map of virtual quantum interactions, which I assert are under the influence of the consciously active information in the energy in the unmanifested state. In the normal or manifested state one would think only of manifested energy in terms of what we know as real matter, and to explain the difference between what tangible matter is and what intangible or unmanifested matter is, I have used Einstein's equation, $E = MC^2$, in which he equates E as energy to MC^2 as matter. If we are to understand that relationship I suggest that the energy in Einstein's equation is intangible, and obviously matter, by definition, is tangible. Swami Rama's yoga diagram describes the process in which intangible or unmanifested energy transforms into physical matter, and in a context of consciousness this process produces tangible matter and the subjective mind.

Patanjali has given us this diagram to explain a form of consciously active information, which Bohm aptly called potential in his Implicate Order. To create a discussion about this process within the unmanifested state of energy, I use the word 'nothing' to represent the singularity present at the end of the compression of the energy in the final moment of a black hole's collapse. This is the same 'nothing' from which Brahma, God, Allah, creates the physical reality.

In this moment/point of the collapse of a black hole, matter has become unmanifested energy, and as a quantum event, that 'nothing' in space has all the information previously related to the matter that is now unmanifested is 'entangled' in a quantum sense in that nothing space. This nothing space is what Patanjali called Prakriti, and the entangled information has become a consciously active entangled quantum potential within Prakriti and that quantum potential manifests as atomic matter because the same active information manifests the standard forces of physics which holds matter in its specific form of solid, liquid or gas.

In physics, this smallest point possible is called the Planck Length, h, described mathematically as 10^{-33}cm. In the Yoga Sutras, Patanjali tells us that the smallest point is 'merely a point without mass.' GS describes that smallest point as a singularity, and the unmanifested energy (Prakriti) as the expansion and collapse of a perpetually oscillating vertical standing waveform in that singularity. What I found to be significant is that in the commentary by Vyasa, Patanjali says that reflection of Purusha by buddhi is referenced against Mahat. GS says the same in Sankhya Karika.

Patanjali tells us that the gunas, Sattva, Tamas and Rajas, are three attributes of the unmanifested energy, Prakriti. Sattva is represents the expansion of the energy, Tamas is its collapse, and Rajas is the activity which is driving the other two gunas. In the description of this oscillation, at the point between the end of one phase of the oscillation and start of the next phase, the unmanifested energy is in a state of equilibrium; in the oscillating phases there is a state of disequilibrium.

GS tells us in Sankhya Karika that the oscillation is perpetual, and for me, this points out that the reader will need to consider each of the phases as individual quantum interactions. The pause between each phase is called Mahat, the greatest Teacher, and is also the reference between Tamas and Sattva in every interaction in Patanjali's spiritual description, and it is equally important in the description of quantum interactions in Sankhya Karika.

At the bottom of the Sattva vector we have evolutes 3-13, which are the mind, with the five cognitive senses and five active senses. At evolutes 14-18, we have five subtle elements, and at 19-23, we have five gross elements with the potential for to having energy manifesting as atomic matter.

GS also suggests that the first four of the five gross elements represent the four standard forces of physics, while the fifth word, space, represents the 'special' space (Akasha), in which the information within the singularity (after its matter has collapsed in the final moment of a black hole) is said to have been retained. Just remember, this is non-physical space in which the retained information (Akasha) is given the title of Greatest Teacher.

This is also where Hawking's Information Paradox[20], *'nothing, not even information, can escape from a black hole,'* can be resolved This information doesn't escape in a physical sense; it is a quantum potential in the black hole's unmanifested energy. The Yoga Sutras go further and say that information can be active across the whole diagram through the intelligent consciousness of purusha, and of course this is the point we need to recognise as Bohm's 'active information.'

This is where my use of Patanjali's word for the creation aspect of consciousness, *Ishvara,* who is 'forever and always free' must be understood. Ishvara is always without a 'distinguishing mark,' 'a special purusha,' in that Ishvara is the Special Conscious Being, and in a temporal sense is lord; a commanding presence. The point to be noted here is that this same active information creates the physical matter in classical physics, according to the 'Laws of physics.'

In a quantum sense the multiple aspects of purusha in the manifested state and unmanifested state are ever present, and referred to with names which, for a yoga teacher or student, infer the relevant state for that action, whether it is creation, knowing, being, et al. Therefore, there can be numerous states of quantum potential simultaneously present in the singularity at a point of space when asymmetry is applied to mind and spacetime; it also applies to classical and quantum physics.

It is reasonable to say the quantum theory recognises this simultaneity as the asymmetry of every quantum interaction of all quantum potentials 'retained' as conscious potentials in all singularities and made available through relativity/context. I can translate asymmetry using the more familiar words of omniscience, omnipresent and omnipotent, and say these are really the attributes of the consciousness of Purusha which reflects on the unmanifested energy of Prakriti.

As a quantum asymmetric state, the singularity will contain all the information related to all the matter that was captured by the black hole, and in its entirety, this information is accessible to Ishvara's consciousness to be known and/or manifested. To make sense of this, I need to make the distinction between the consciousness of Ishvara and mind.

This distinction will only be evident in the Samadhi or Siddhi state, and in yoga this 'knowledge' is called 'direct experience,' meaning it is the person's direct experience of Ishvara's observation of that moment, which is the 'apprehension' referred to in YS 1.11. We find that mind is a product of the process of creating matter, whereas there is only one real consciousness; that of Purusha, which, on reflecting on the unmanifested energy of Prakriti, becomes the conscious mind, albeit in a state of ignorance.

The consciousness of Ishvara is independent of the body in its use of the 'retained information' in space/Akasha, and the best description of that process was written by my friend, the late Dr Syamala Hari, in a collaborative essay we authored in the Quantum Dream Journal, and I am grateful to Dr Huping Hu, of Quantum Dream, for giving me permission to incorporate that essay in this book and I will place that work in its own Chapter.

CHAPTER 9

A 'normal' friend's perspective

This article was written in collaboration with a dear friend who gave me a lot of intellectual support; the friend is the late Dr Syamala Hari, PhD., who was an authority on the subject of Artificial Intelligence and Hindu philosophy. I was fortunate to have her as a friend and mentor, but especially as the scientist with whom I collaborated to interpret my Samapatti experiences for an article we submitted to a panel of academics, set up by Quantum Dream in reference to retained information.

That article, "Body-Independence of Consciousness and Retained Information," is her clinically focused scientist's mind, writing from a scientist's perspective, of what I have written in the previous chapters. I take this opportunity to share with you her perspective on my Samapatti experiences, and how they can be explained and understood.

Body-Independence of Consciousness and 'Retained' Information[22]
Alan J Oliver and Syamala D Hari.

ABSTRACT

In ancient times, Hindu philosophy thoroughly analysed consciousness, mind, body, and their relations to one another. The philosophy asserts that consciousness is independent of both body and mind, where mind means the accumulation of experiences, desires, aversion, emotions, etc. of a living being. Hence it asserts that consciousness does not end, nor awaken, nor transform with bodily death but continues unaffected. According to this philosophy, mind is not conscious just like lifeless matter but mind can interact with matter in suitable conditions. The theory of mind-brain interactions in Hindu philosophy may be called interactive dualism but it is NOT Cartesian dualism. We present experiences of one of the authors (Oliver's), of a conscious but thoughtless state called Samapatti, as examples to support the view that consciousness is not produced by the body. Oliver got into the Samapatti state whenever he focussed his mind on a human or animal subject; in that state, his mind became still and then he became aware of some physical or psychological conditions of his subject. These experiences show that one can be conscious without the usual in-and-out thought flow and be aware of something external to one's own body and mind without any physical or sensory connection. We point out that these apparently 'anomalous', experiences are possible realities described in the traditional sources of Hindu Philosophy. Since the topic of consciousness inevitably includes what one is conscious or aware of, we also discussed whether the information content of experiences accumulated during the life of a living being disappears after death, or whether at least some of it remains. Interestingly, today's researches in near-death experiences and reincarnation seem to validate Hindu philosophy's propositions that consciousness is not produced by the body or brain and that some mental contents survive bodily death (as implied by the so-called principle of reincarnation).

Key words: Consciousness, Body and Mind, Samadhi, Samapatti, Bhagavad Gita, Yoga Sutras of Patanjali, Reincarnation, Near Death Experiences.

1. Introduction

The question, "Does consciousness end, continue, awaken, or transform when the body dies?" is one that occupied the minds of prominent thinkers of all civilizations ever since ancient times. Interest in finding answers to this question continues even today as seen from the growing literature on reincarnation, near-death experiences (NDEs), out-of-body-experiences (OBEs), and other paranormal phenomena. To answer the above question in its various aspects the authors have turned to personal experiences in the Samadhi and Samapatti states and to explanations from the Hindu traditional philosophies in Bhagavad Gita and the Yoga Sutras of Patanjali, because these sources analysed relations among consciousness, mind, and body thoroughly. Interestingly, today's researches in NDEs, OBEs, and reincarnation seem to validate Hindu philosophy's propositions that consciousness is not produced by the body or brain and that some mental contents survive bodily death (as implied by the so-called principle of reincarnation).

Phenomenal information (PI), the content of a conscious experience: In our lives, we have many conscious experiences. In any such experience, there is awareness of something, which may be an emotion, a desire, a thought etc., or awareness of seeing, hearing, touching, tasting, or smelling an external object accessed by one's senses. We may call this something information. There seems to be a subject, which we report as 'I' and there is ability to be aware, which seems to be available when we are awake but not in deep sleep; in dream sleep, there is ability to be aware of some imaginations but not of the sensory contacts with the outside world. Hence a conscious experience has three components to it: 1) the 'I', 2) some 'phenomenal information (why we add the qualifier, 'phenomenal' will be explained in the following paragraphs), and 3) the act of knowing or being aware.

In the case of a sensory experience, for example, seeing an apple, this information is different from both the apple and its biological/ neural map created in the brain/body of the human (living) being. It is useful to note this difference because according to modern neuroscience, every subjective (conscious) state such as a conscious intention or conscious emotion, or perception of an external object, occurs only if a required and correlated neural process takes place. Each conscious state has its associated neural correlates of consciousness: one for seeing a red patch, another one for seeing grandmother, yet a third one for hearing a siren, etc. (Mormann and Koch 2007). Interestingly, one is never aware of the existence of the neural correlate (NC) in one's own brain. One is only aware of the NC's 'meaning', which must have been created along with the NC. In contrast, a neuroscientist monitoring the brain can see an image of the NC on the monitor but does not directly know the NC's 'meaning' (namely, what the owner of the brain is aware of). The neuroscientist will have to accept whatever the brain's owner reports as his/her experience.

Phenomenal information is different from matter. We (human beings) can report our conscious experiences to others if we wish to do so. When we do, we use a language and any of several means: sounds, electrical signals, write on a paper, and so on. Every means of communication requires human (living) beings to ASSIGN meaning or information that is in our heads (which we called PI), to structures of matter or material energy. These structures carry a mapping of the PI; the structures themselves are not identical with the Pl [i]. Yet, in our daily lives, we do not distinguish between PI and the means we use to communicate or store it outside our heads. For example, we say "the book has good information about the city", whereas the book only has words whose meanings exist in our heads but not in the book. Hence modern scientists called the information, which a living being is aware of in an experience 'phenomenal information' to emphasize that it is different from the language or energy signals used for its storage and communication or the corresponding neural/biological activity in the body.

Fortunately for us, no means of communication, or information storage device, or a computer ever creates or assigns any new PI overwriting what we intended it to carry! Hence, we may assume that lifeless matter does not create PI all by itself. On the other hand, as long as we are awake, we experience more and more, thereby keep on accumulating more PI in our memory and this memory has two components: biological and mental. The mental component consists of PI; the biological component is what a monitoring instrument can convey physically/scientifically. We have to infer that the living matter in brain/body not only creates a biophysical map of a material object accessed by its senses but also creates a 'meaning' of the map, i.e., the associated Pl.

PI is subjective. It is every day experience that one's thoughts cannot be seen, heard, etc., by others, i.e., by their senses, nor can they be accessed by any material instruments; one's thoughts are not known to others unless one conveys them verbally or by other physical means (making it very tempting to lie!). We call this inaccessibility of the mind by senses and material devices subjectivity2

PI is different from consciousness. One may ask "are phenomenal information (PI) and the ability to know different, or is consciousness a property of the former?" Many Western philosophers (for example, Descartes) do not see a distinction between the mind and consciousness whereas in Hindu and Buddhist philosophies, mind (an accumulation of PI) is said to be not conscious just like lifeless matter and to be different from consciousness! However even in the West, Leibniz, Helmholtz, Kant, and psychologists including William James, Sigmund Freud, and many others discussed existence of unconscious thought at length (Kihlstrom 1994). More recently, modern psychologists found evidence for unconscious thought and unconscious cognition[3]. Hence, we may assume that PI and the ability to know are different, and that consciousness is not a property of PI.

Now, from the point of view of physics, the body of a living being is made of the same fundamental particles of which lifeless matter is made. While lifeless matter outside any living body does not seem to create PI, every human body seems to be creating more and more experiences and accumulating PI in the wakeful and dream states. Since we all know that living matter inevitably becomes lifeless some time or other, the questions, "what happens to the PI accumulated until death and what happens to consciousness, i.e., the ability to know, which was there until death?" naturally arise. Answers to these questions are clearly very difficult to address by scientific means because both PI and consciousness are subjective. Some scientists simply assume that matter exists in two kinds of states: one living and the other lifeless, and that PI and consciousness are properties of living matter and therefore those properties disappear with change of state by death. Yet, since it is only an assumption so far but not yet proved by any scientific means, the possibility that consciousness and/or some or all of the PI accumulated during life survive/s death does exist.

To explore that possibility in its various aspects, in this article, we turn to personal experiences in the Samadhi and Samapatti states described in traditional sources of Hindu philosophies such as Bhagavadgita and Yoga Sutras of Patanjali. We also cite some experiments of Bevan Reid, a distinguished medical scientist, who seemed to have found evidence of an etheric field in his laboratory space which could retain some "experiences" of living cells even after their death. We also point out that some prominent modern researchers of reincarnation, NDE, and OBE seem to agree with Hindu philosophy's principle of reincarnation and the view that consciousness is not produced by the body or brain.

In the following sections, we will describe how Hindu philosophy's dualistic theory of mind-body interactions explains why mind is not accessible to senses.

[2] Unconscious cognition is the processing of perception, memory, learning, thought, and language without being aware of it. The role of the unconscious mind on decision making is a topic greatly debated by neuroscientists, linguists and psychologists around the world. (https://en.wikipedia.org/wiki/Unconscious cognition).

Bhagavadgita and Yoga Sutras of Patanjali. We also cite some experiments of Bevan Reid, a distinguished medical scientist, who seemed to have found evidence of an etheric field in his laboratory space which could retain some "experiences" of living cells even after their death. We also point out that some prominent modern researchers of reincarnation, NDE, and OBE seem to agree with Hindu philosophy's principle of reincarnation and the view that consciousness is not produced by the body or brain.

2. Does Consciousness End, or Continue, When the Body Dies?

Hindu philosophy's answer to the above question is that consciousness continues unaffected; it is universal and fundamental and not altered by the death of an individual's body. A very brief summary of some of the teachings in Bhagavad Gita is as follows:

- There exists Universal Consciousness, which is omnipresent, omniscient, and omnipotent.
- Every living being is associated with its own soul (Jiva) which is a part of that infinite Consciousness, who draws to itself the senses and the mind that are part of Nature (Bhagavad Gita Chapter 15, verse 7). Being part of the eternal Consciousness, the soul is eternal also and survives the death of the physical body.
- The Self (Atman) is Consciousness seated in the hearts of all beings (Bhagavad Gita chapter 10, verse 20).
- Kenopanishad (Swami, 1920) says that the mind and senses are able to perform their respective functions willed and supported by Consciousness; without Consciousness, the senses and the mind cannot function.
- The mind consists of ego (ahamkara), ability to think (manas), desires, aversion, emotions, experiences, etc. (chitta), and intellect (buddhi) which includes the ability to make decisions based on memory.
- Bhagavadgita describes the distinctions between the body mind complex and the one who 'knows' them (shetrajna). The Field (shetra) consists of the body, the senses and sense objects, the body's environment (Nature), and the mind.

Nature includes the five elements: earth, water, fire, air and the sky, and the five senses: hearing, touching, seeing, tasting and smelling; objects of the senses are sound, touch, form and color, taste and smell.

- All contents of the Field, namely, the body, its environment, and the mind are said to be insentient (Bhagavad Gita, 7:4).

- The knower of the Field (shetrajna) is Consciousness Himself and His infinitesimal projection, Jiva who assumed this function within this body. As to the interaction of the body and the mind, in the chapter called Karma Yoga, Gita says that the senses influence the body, and manas and chitta influence the senses; buddhi influences the manas and chitta, and Jiva influences buddhi.

- The senses and the mind cannot grasp Consciousness, and no scientific theory can logically prove His existence (Kenopanishad), and therefore no scientific experiments can detect Him either. The same thing is true about Jiva.

Individual consciousness perceived in living beings differs from Universal Consciousness (we call this Consciousness with a big C in front) in that the former is fragmented. An individual's consciousness exists only in wakeful and dreaming sleep states and knows only one thing at a time and in general, one individual usually does not know the conscious experience of another whereas Universal consciousness knows everything everywhere all the time! It is explained in Hindu philosophy why each individual mind appears to be conscious. It is because the Universal Consciousness creates a reflection (pratibimba) as it were, in each mind and this reflection is the 'I' thought called ahamkara in Sanskrit and appears to be conscious; it is the individual consciousness.

Mind is faster than matter — Subjectivity of mind: Some Hindu philosophers may say that mind is subtle matter. This statement is an abridgement of the following: that mind is not accessible to senses, that it is as insentient as lifeless matter, and that the body and the mind interact with, and influence each other throughout life. The statement should not be understood to mean that mind is the same as, or a state of the physical matter, which sciences such as physics and chemistry have studied so far. Modern science deals with matter which is accessible to senses directly or indirectly via material instruments. By asserting mind's inaccessibility to senses, Hindu philosophy posits mind as different from gross physical matter or even material energy; for example, the so-called principle of reincarnation depends upon the proposition that some mental contents called vasanas or samskaras survive bodily death.

In Hindu philosophy, 'mind control' is a major topic. It is often said that one who can keep the mind free of all thoughts can see for oneself the true nature[1] of consciousness. Controlling the mind is recognized as a difficult task and various techniques are prescribed to 'control' the mind. It is emphasized that the mind is restless and cannot come to a stop (it is a common experience that thoughts keep rising one after another when one is awake or in the dream state). The mind is described as being very fast, faster than the senses, faster

---

[1]   Consciousness or Atma when it is joined to nature, appears to feel either pleasure or pain. Whenever an event or object is perceived a thought-wave (vritti) raises in the mind. Ahamkara, the ego-sense identifies itself with this wave. This false identification is the cause of all our misery. One cannot recognize one's real Self as long as this false identification exists. An analogy explains this. If the water in a lake is muddy or is agitated, the bottom cannot be seen. If the water is clear, and there are no waves, we see the bottom. So with the mind; when it is calm, we see what our own nature is; we do not mix our self but remain our own selves. Hence Hindu philosophy teaches many techniques to bring the mind to stillness.

than physical matter and material energy, and faster than anything in the physical world, in other words, faster than light. It is our everyday experience that our minds are subjective. Clearly, Hindu philosophy explains why mind is subjective; the energy which physical senses can grasp is limited by the speed of light and therefore senses cannot grasp something that is faster than light.

Interestingly, assuming the theme that mind is faster than matter, mind brain interactions can be described as tachyon interaction with ordinary non-relativistic matter. This mathematical model of mind-brain interaction is interactive dualism and shows how the brain creates PI (subjective experience) if the mind pays attention to the brain (Hari 2011). This model also explains why every subjective experience (including remembering a past experience) happens 'now' in one's mind (Hari 2016). This model was successful in explaining and justifying Eccles's hypothesis about the role of volition in exocytosis, the basic process of inter-neuronal communication (Hari 2008), and Libet's causal anomalies (Hari 2014).

Living being — computer analogy: Descriptions of Consciousness, mind, and body and their relations summarized above may be better understood using the following analogy: The physical body of a living being is like a piece of hardware. It is made up of matter. Every living being, human or animal, or any living organism (possibly excluding some primitive forms of life), has an accumulation of experiences, desires, aversion, emotions, etc., and therefore an accumulation of information, in other words a memory, which we is called mind in this paper. In this sense, mind is like a computer memory containing data and programs. Just like a computer's hardware and software do not know what they are doing, their own existence, and the meaning of their memory contents, both the body and the mind of a living being also do not really know anything but there is a certain Consciousness (apart from the mind mentioned above) that "knows". Consciousness is like the computer operator, as it were, and the one who "really knows" everything that is part of the living being's activity. The ability to think (logical reasoning), and the ability to make decisions based on existing contents are similar to computer programs in that they can exist in an active or a passive state. They create new PI (what one is aware of in a new experience) by being active; after new PI is created they remain in the memory in a passive state until they are called upon for action again.

> The mind and the body are both not conscious just like the hardware and software of a computer. Only Consciousness and soul really know and have control over all that happens in an individual's life. Mind is subtle and its magic is visible only when it is working with the body similar to the way the capabilities of software (also subtle) are visible only when it is loaded into the computer and activated.

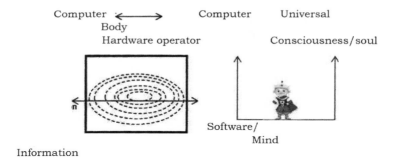

Figure 1. Computer analogy of Consciousness, Mind, and Body Relations in Vedanta

Oliver's Samapatti seems to indicate that consciousness is independent of the body and the mind. Samapatti is a conscious state, where there are no thoughts flowing in and out. In the Patanjali's Yoga tradition[s], Samapatti would be classified as a Siddhi, a capability gained through the application of Samadhi, a state of consciousness which is attained through meditation and which lies beyond waking, dreaming, or deep sleep. Samadhi may be attained by single-pointed concentration that slows down mental activity to a complete stop. When Oliver focused his mind on a human or animal subject, he entered the Samapatti state and became aware of some physical and psychological conditions of the subject. All his subjects experienced peace as their anxieties gradually cleared during the session. In that state, Oliver could see and know beyond our normal experience of knowing; he did not need a physical connection to the subject to know the subject's state of mind. After reading the Yoga Sutras of Patanjali he found a description of Samadhi in Yoga Sutra 1.41 and that his state of mind in his healing sessions would be called Samapatti (one kind of Samadhi) according to the sutras. Let us now recall some of Oliver's Samapatti experiences as a healer (Oliver 2010). In a later section, we will see that they match the description of Samadhi by the Yoga Sutras.

[5] Oliver's quest for understanding his own experiences led him to a branch of the Hindu philosophy because most Western philosophies do not see a distinction between thought and consciousness whereas in Hindu and Buddhist philosophies, the mind is said to be not conscious just like lifeless matter. as their anxieties gradually cleared during the session. In that state, Oliver could see and know beyond our normal experience of seeing and knowing; he did not need a physical connection to the subject to know the subject's state of mind. After reading the Yoga Sutras of Patanjali he found a description of Samadhi, in Yoga Sutra 1.41 and that his state of mind in his healing sessions would be called Samapatti (one kind of Samadhi) according to the Sutras. Let us now recall some of Oliver's Samapatti

experiences as a healer (Oliver 2010). In a later section, we will see that they match the description of Samadhi by the Yoga Sutras.

In one instance, Oliver's subject was a disturbed cat which was antisocial and hadn't washed itself for more than a year. As he focused on it with closed eyes, his mind became still. He became aware that the cat went to sleep and had chaotic visual images, a bit like multiple auras of migraine. He then felt that the chaos cleared to become a garden scene viewed from cat eyelevel, with very large plants and shades of brown, yellow and red colors. At the same time, he was also aware that he had never seen the garden before and that the images were not in his own mind but that he watched the cat's dream. After a while, when Oliver felt that the cat would wake up, it woke up and began to wash itself suggesting that the disturbances in its mind subsided during the Samapatti session. In another instance, Oliver fixed his mind on the fractured leg of a lady waiting for a bone graft. Once again his mind attained stillness and he became aware of the physical distress within the bone. He silently wished to replace the distress which he felt was dark, with something bright and vibrant like gold. When he opened his eyes, she told him with excitement that she visualized bright gold energy replacing some black stuff in the bone. A week later, she had the leg x-rayed in preparation for a bone graft; the x-ray showed new bone growth at the fracture site. There is an interesting point here: Normally (if not in Sampatti), Oliver is unable to visualize anything. That the lady visualized the wish of Oliver while he was in Sampatti, and reported the visualization to him after the session, confirmed to him that in the case of the session with the cat, the garden scene was the dream of the cat and not his visualization or hallucination.

One common aspect of all Sampatti experiences of Oliver is that while he was in the state of stillness, those anxieties, disturbances, perturbations, etc., that were there earlier in his subject's mind gradually cleared and the subject's mind also became still. For instance, he worked over some years with a lady called Emma, who had breast cancer and helped her to come to terms with whatever the outcome might be. Samapatti sessions were her favourites because when he went into stillness her pain and her concern for herself stopped as she too became still and thereby peaceful. Another person who suffered from Huntington's chorea was helped by Oliver using Samapatti. His uncontrollable movements ceased for the duration of the session, typically around 45 minutes. Since the random movements ceased while he was asleep, as is the nature of the disease, obviously during the Sampatti session this person's mind and brain also calmed down similar enough to mimic sleep, although he was awake.

In all his Samapatti sessions, Oliver was aware of his own state of mind as well as that of his subject's and was able to know which was his own and which was the subject's. The explanation from Hindu philosophy for this experience is as follows (Hari and Oliver 2015): once the seer disconnects his/her identification with his/her body by focusing on the subject, he/she is in the thoughtless state with no ahamkara and raises to the level of Consciousness in Figure 1, the operator of all computers. Just as a computer operator can see the contents of two computers, Consciousness can see the memory contents of both individuals, the seer and the subject, and know that anxiety is in the subject's memory but not in the seer's memory. Again like the computer operator, Consciousness can enter this fact into the seer's memory; Consciousness could also remove anxious thoughts and hyperactivity in the subject's minds and make them peaceful during the session. Ordinary living beings who cannot break their identification with the body and mind cannot exchange their memory contents without using senses just like computers cannot communicate without a material connection. The common aspects of Oliver's Sampatti sessions and the sequence of events in a typical session are presented pictorially in Figure 2.

Computer I : Seer's mind/memory

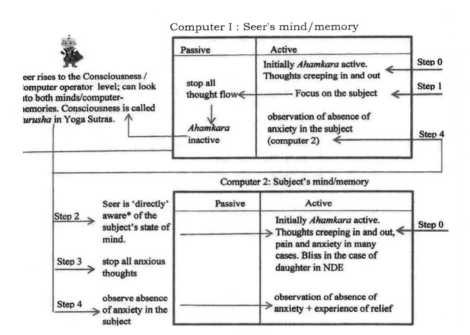

* Seer is like a piece of crystal before flowers; the crystal becomes almost identified with flowers. If the flower is red, the crystal looks red, or if the flower is blue, the crystal looks blue. It is the beyond-sensory perception of samadhi that grasps the true nature of an object in reality, absolutely free from the distortions of our imagination. Samadhi is, in fact, much more than perception; it is direct knowledge.

Figure 2. A pictorial representation of sequence of events in Samapatti

Experiences such as above show that one can remain conscious although the usual thought flow in one's mind has stopped. They also show that one (the seer) could know another's mind without requiring a physical connection, which ability is beyond our normal knowing experience. They make one wonder whether real Consciousness is distinct from what we usually see and call consciousness in living beings. These seemingly impossible events suggest that Consciousness must be something quite distinct from the brain and its memory/PI. If one's ability to know is independent of one's brain, it would follow that the ability does not cease to exist when the body dies.

Near-Death Experiences (NDE) indicate that consciousness and mind exist independently of the body. Nowadays, there is growing interest among scientists in NDE research as they hear reports from hospitals that patients who have been declared clinically dead exhibited various mental capabilities such as cognition, perception, and memory with enhanced mental clarity under cerebral impairment conditions such as cardiac arrest and general anaesthesia, when such mental activity cannot be associated with normal brain function. An example of enhanced mental functioning during an NDE is a rapid revival with exceptional clarity of memories that extends over the person's entire life. Researchers call one type of experience as veridical NDE, in which experiencers acquire verifiable information that they could not have obtained by any normal means. For example, some experiencers reported seeing events going on at some distant location, such as another room of the hospital while they are unconscious. Some reported visions of deceased persons, including those not previously known to be deceased, and it was found later that the demises had actually happened.

A common feature of near-death or after death experiences is the remarkable clarity of their reports surpassing those of normal waking state. In some NDE, the experiencers even acquired information which they could not have obtained by any normal means but which was indeed verified to be true later on. Greyson (2011) argues that if the mind is solely dependent on the brain for its existence, clarity of mental activity should be diminishing in clinical death conditions, and knowledge of events without the required sensory inputs would be impossible. In his view, these features of NDEs indicate that mind may only be dependent on the brain much as a radio transmission is dependent upon a receiver and broadcast unit but mind is not dependent on the brain to the extent that it cannot exist or function when the brain cannot function. Greyson thinks that the observed correlation between brain states and mind states is compatible with the theory that mind is produced by the brain, but it is also compatible with the theory that the brain may be a vehicle which receives, transports, and transmits, but is not synonymous with the mind.

Greyson's view of the brain-mind relationship is compatible with our view of it, namely, that the relation is similar to the hardware-software relationship in a computer (Hari 2015). We think that the brain plays the role of hardware and the mind plays the role of the software in creating new experience/information. Information stored in a computer is of two kinds: data and programs. The former are passive. Any program is of the latter kind; it is passive until it is activated. Once activated, the program runs and creates outputs which are new records/information in the memory. To do even the simple task of creating a record of any input, the computer needs to have a "WRITE" instruction, a program, already in its memory.

The input activates the stored program, which then runs in the hardware (i.e., the hardware goes through a dynamic process) and creates passive records. After the activity is over, the program goes back to its passive state. The point to note is that hardware does not produce new records all by itself; it takes both hardware and software to do so. Similarly, to produce a new experience, a thinking activity, which is an interaction of already existing thoughts with the biological matter, needs to take place in the brain. New mental records are produced as a result of the process. The activity may be initiated by a desire/purpose (thoughts), or by sensory inputs, the soul or by Consciousness. Similar to a computer program, at the end of a thinking activity which involves both body and mind, those mental contents which participated in the activity still remain passively in the memory[6]. Again, the main point to note here is that the brain does not create new information all by itself; it needs to interact with already stored information/mind to produce the new information. Like hardware and software in a computer, brain and mind are not identical. The brain serves as the receiver of sensory inputs for creating sensory experience and as the broadcast unit for communicating its mind (stored information) to others.

Thus, like Samapatti experiences, NDEs also indicate that both consciousness and mind exist independent of the body and therefore suggest the possibility of their survival after bodily death.

3. Does the information accumulated until death survive death? Reincarnation

Having noted that the mind/PI of a brain is different from the brain although the brain plays a role in creating the PI, one may ask what happens to the PI accumulated until death. Hindu philosophy's answer to this question is that the accumulated information remains after death.

The theory of mind-brain interactions in Hindu philosophy may be called interactive dualism because while recognizing both mind's action upon the body and the body/brain's role in creating experience, mind is considered neither as a state of the biological matter in the body nor as an emergent property of it but. The contents of mind are said to be faster than matter and light implying that they are different from organic or inorganic matter. In fact, the basis for the well-known principle of reincarnation is that some mental contents called vasanas or samskaras survive bodily death. However, this theory is NOT Cartesian Dualism because the philosophy affirms the existence of a supreme Consciousness and an individual Jiva who are immaterial; they are beyond the mind. The ego (the I-feeling called ahamkara) is part of the mind and not conscious. Hence neither Jiva nor the ego is the 'I' of Descartes who presumes that the mind, the 'I', and soul are more or less the same thing and that it is conscious.

[6] For example, a violinist has the ability to play the violin but he/she does not play the violin all the time. The ability to play violin is stored in the musician's memory in a passive state and he/she activates it to perform. He/she enjoys the music while playing violin and remembers the experience even afterwards. After the performance is done, the ability to play violin is still there and no one else knows about the musician's talent unless he/she performs.

In Hindu philosophy, life is the process of interaction between the body and the mind (in the computer analogy, this interaction is similar to execution of software in the hardware). Life begins when mind starts interacting with the body and lasts as long as the interaction continues. At death, the body is no longer able to support the interaction (just like a computer with defective hardware does not support software execution). Further, the philosophy proposes that some accumulated latent impressions of all past experiences, and desires called vasanas or samskaras survive the death of the physical body and carried by the immortal Jiva into a new life[2] if the Jiva is not yet detached from them and therefore not liberated but bound to experience consequences of actions in previous lives. The new life gives vasanas another chance for expression. This is the principle of reincarnation believed in Hindu and other Eastern philosophies and religions and not found in Western philosophies and religions. This principle does not appear too unreasonable because it is similar to the following scenario involving a computer's software and hardware: a computer with broken hardware cannot run a piece of software which if saved on a storage device, can be entered into another computer and made to run again!

Today, reincarnation is the subject of recent investigations by many parapsychologists, psychics, and even psychiatrists. Belief in the reality of reincarnation is gaining support even from scientists such as Carr (a physicist) and Smythies (a neuroscientist). One of the noteworthy researches on this topic is by Stevenson, who was a Professor of Psychiatry and Director or the Division of Perceptual Studies at the University of Virginia. He compiled and studied voluminous data that appear to provide scientific proof that reincarnation is real. In one of his books (Stevenson 1967), he shows by scientific reasoning why reincarnation is the only viable explanation that fits the facts of his study. He was able to rule out alternative explanations for

---

[2]   In Aphorism 2.9, Patanjali says that the desire to cling to life is inherent both in the ignorant and in the learned. This is because the mind retains impressions of the death experience from many previous incarnations; after all, how could we fear death so much if we had never previously experienced it?

his twenty cases of young children who were spontaneously able to describe events in a previous life as soon as they learned to talk. His study is also reproducible by any sceptic so that doubts about the validity of his study can be eliminated. Stevenson's later research further supported the reality of reincarnation because he travelled to the scenes reported in past-life accounts and interviewed witnesses to assess details provided in the accounts. In over 1000 of these cases, the past lives of these children could be factually validated.

If information about past lives is remembered by someone then in the time interval between any two of that someone's lives, the information must exist somewhere and not be destroyed. Where it is stored must be a non-physical medium because in that interval, it is not accessible to other living beings with normal sensory capabilities.

4. Where the information surviving death is retained

We said mind is a store of PI. During life, one's mind is obviously intimately linked with one's body because any ailments or impairments of the body are necessarily accompanied by corresponding defects in one's memory and ability to experience. So, once the body dies and is no longer able to report any piece of information, the assumption that information is not destroyed but remains, raises the question "where is the surviving information retained?" Patanjali's Yoga Sutras seem to have an answer for this question. The Sutras also say who is able to find/read/know that retained information.

Figure 3 illustrates cosmology according to the Sankhya philosophy which is part of the Yoga Philosophy. Samkhya states that the whole universe evolves from two sources: consciousness, or Purusha, the eternal reality, the real Self, Atman in Sanskrit; and nature, or Prakriti, pure creative power. Within Prakriti are the three fundamental forces: tamas, inertia and ignorance; rajas, momentum and desire; and sativa, balance, luminosity, and knowledge. They make up the Prakriti and are important principally as physio-psychological +factors. The first stage of evolution from undifferentiated Prakriti is called Mahat, "the great cause" occurs when Prakriti is illuminated by the spiritual light of a Purusha. Mahat is universal intelligence, and each human mind is a part of that cosmic intelligence. From Mahat evolves individual buddhi, the discriminating faculty. From buddhi evolves ahamkara, the individual ego-sense. From ahamkara, the lines of evolution branch off in three different directions—to produce manas, the recording faculty; the five powers of perception (sight, smell, hearing, taste and touch); the five organs of action (tongue, feet, hands and the organs of evacuation and procreation); and the five tanmatras, which are the subtle inner essences of sound, feelings, aspect, flavor and odour. These subtle tanmatras, combining and recombining, are then said to produce the five gross elements of which the external universe is composed: earth, water, fire, air or gas including breath and Prana, and space (Akasha).

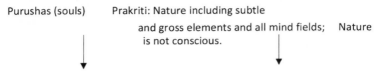

Ishvara/God is special Purusha untouched by ignorance and the products of ignorance, not subject to karmas or samskaras or the results of action.

Purushas (souls)   Prakriti: Nature including subtle

and gross elements and all mind fields;   Nature
is not conscious.

Mahat: the first to evolve from Prakriti and first vehicle of a Purusha in its interaction with Prakriti; it is the faculty of discrimination and subtle energy that will create and called universal intelligence or Universal Mind.

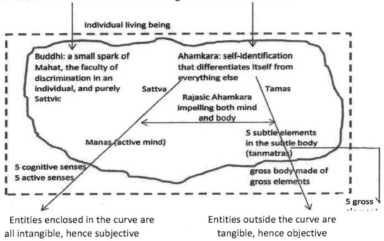

Entities enclosed in the curve are all intangible, hence subjective

Entities outside the curve are tangible, hence objective

Figure 3. The Yoga perspective of creation

Purushas or souls are infinite in number and similar but separate, none superior to any other. Purusha is not the doer but the witness. Experience is explained on the basis of a certain association of Purusha with nature. Nature is merely the medium for Purusha to manifest itself; Nature is not the source of consciousness. The mind seems to be intelligent and conscious whereas it has only a borrowed intelligence. Knowledge or perception is a thought-wave (vritti) in the mind. Since the mind is not the seer, but only an instrument of knowledge, it is also an object of perception like the outside world. The Atman is the real seer. Thus, to summarize, creation is described as an evolution outward, from undifferentiated into differentiated consciousness, from cosmic mind into universe. Pure consciousness is, as it were, gradually covered by successive layers of ignorance and differentiation, each layer being grosser and thicker than the one below it, until the process ends on the outer physical surface of the visible and tangible world (Swami Prabhvaananda).

False identification, right knowledge or Self-Realization: Purusha, when it is joined to nature, appears to feel either pleasure or pain. When an event or object is perceived, a thought-wave raises in the mind. Ahamkara, the ego-sense identifies itself with this wave. This false identification is the cause of all our misery; even the ego's temporary sensation of happiness brings anxiety, a desire to cling to the object of pleasure, and this prepares future possibilities of becoming unhappy. Although Atman remains forever outside the power of thought-waves, one can never know one's real Self as long as thought-waves and the ego-sense are being identified. To explain this, the commentators employ a simple analogy. If the water in a lake is muddy, the bottom will not be seen, or it is agitated all the time, the bottom will not be seen. If the water is clear, and there are no waves, we shall see the bottom. So with the mind; when it is calm, we see what our own nature is; we do not mix our self but remain our own selves. Hence Patanjali speaks of techniques of "control of thought-waves" at length[8].

Hindu philosophy believes in cycles of creation. The whole universe is composed of two materials, Akasha and Prana. Akasha is the omnipresent, all-penetrating existence. Everything that has form is evolved out of this Akasha. All force, whether gravitation, attraction or repulsion, or life, is the outcome of one primal force called Prana. Prana acting on Akasha creates or projects the universe. At the beginning of a cycle, there is only this Akasha and it is motionless and unmanifested. Then Prana begins to act, more and more, creating grosser and grosser forms out of Akasha: plants, animals, humans, stars, and so on. At the end of the cycle, all contents of the universe melt into the Akasha again, and the next creation similarly proceeds out of this Akasha. Both Akasha and Prana are incorporated into Mahat (Swami Vivekananda). Mahat, which is the Cosmic Mind, one may say, is the Cosmic Computer that stores memories and impressions as well as governs the many senses and limbs, in other words, the machinery of the Cosmos. Whatever happens or has occurred in the past is stored in Mahat, in a manner that we may back-up files onto a computer and place them away. Only when we open or access them, do we have knowledge of them. This is the same basic way that Mahat also works (Lingham 2013).

Parts of Chapter 3 (Vibhuti Pada) of Yoga Sutras are used by Alice Bailey as proof of existence of Akashic Records (Trine 2010). Bailey wrote in her book Light of the Soul on The Yoga Sutras of Patanjali — Book 3 (Bailey 1927): "The Akashic record is like an immense photographic film, registering all the desires and earth experiences of our planet. Those who perceive it will see pictured thereon: The life experiences of every human being since time began, the reactions to experience of the entire animal kingdom, the aggregation of the thought-forms of a karmic nature (based on desire) of every human unit throughout time."

[8] Pursuing the analogy of the lake (Swami Prabhvaananda), let us consider banks of sand or pebbles built by waves by their continued action, at the lake bottom. They are more permanent and solid than the waves themselves. They may be compared to the tendencies, potentialities and latent states, which exist in the subconscious and

unconscious areas of the mind. They are called *samskaras*. *Samskaras* are built up by the continued action of thought-waves and drive our actions. Another name for the carried over experience of an individual soul is Karma. A mental or physical act is called karma. *Karma* is also used to describe the consequence of an act, and hence to describe the sum of the consequences of our past actions in this and previous lives. Since *samskaras* drive actions and actions in their turn, produce new thought-waves, *samskaras* and Karma form an endless cycle. Yoga philosophy teaches us that it is the *samskaras* that drive us from birth to birth just as a strongly rooted addiction drives man to take a drug, over and over again.

Oliver was 'born that way': As said earlier, in all his experiences in the state of Samapatti, Oliver was aware of his own state of mind as well as that of his subject's and was able to know which was his own and which was that of the subject. This led to him asking himself where this ability came from since he had not received any specific training in that regard. Oliver found from Yoga Sutras that there are only two ways to become established in Samadhi.

1. A lifetime of study and meditation with an accredited teacher, or
2. To be 'born that way'.

The Samapatti experiences of Oliver raise a significant point in relation to the retention of information after death. If one is born that way (established in that state of Samadhi), it means that the ability or tendency to get into Samadhi must be arising from the experience and skill acquired in an earlier life. That is to say, the Samadhi was a skill and a samskara that is retained at the level of Mahai.

Bevan Reid and etheric fields (Jacka 2011): In 1986, a colleague of Oliver, Bevan Reid, conducted experiments on mouse fibroblast cultures in a bovine solution as part of his cancer research. Although he did not work directly with the human energy field, his work does have interesting implications for the possibility of retaining human experiences in space. First, Reid found that cell cultures grown in the presence of a mass of 10kg of lead had a shorter life span that was the norm. Then after removing the lead from the laboratory space, he found that fresh cell cultures still died at this accelerated rate. This effect on fresh cell cultures lasted for weeks (Lasting of the effect could be due to radiation from lead still remaining the laboratory space.) During these experiments, Reid placed some glass slides coated with polystyrene some distance away from the cell cultures and allowed the slides to dry. An almost identical copy of the cells was produced on the plain polystyrene and illustrated action at a distance and the possibility of the transmission of biological data through a subtle field without any physical contact.

Purusha who is in the state of ignorance by mistakenly identifying itself with aspects of *Prakriti* is equivalent to *Jiva* in the terminology of Bhagavad Gita. Right knowledge is Self-realisation by *Purusha's* withdrawal from this false identification. As seen from the lake analogy, both good and bad *karma* impede the journey of *Jiva* towards its ultimate Self-realisation. In various religions this realisation is associated with Heaven, God, both or neither. The Yoga Sutras prescribe ways to put an end to the false identification, one of the ways being devotion to God (*Ishvara)*. Patanjali introduces the idea of God into Sankhya. *Ishvara* is the special kind of Purusha, untouched by ignorance and the products of ignorance, not subject to *karmas* or *samskaras* or the results of action.

Reid concluded that some force was coming through space producing these affects related to bacteria. Polystyrene coated slides had the image of a cell, exact in its detail to the extent that it even included the same staining as in the earlier cell cultures. (In the first experiment, cells were stained to produce enough contrast when viewed through the microscope.) Reid assumed that the staining agent caused some trauma to the cells (an experience/affect, which he called insult to the cell). Tiny vortices were found to have formed in the polystyrene as it dried. Reid thought that vortices appeared when form is imprinted on matter. In his experiments, he saw a continuous interaction between space and matter. He envisaged the outflow from matter to produce an exact copy of the form and that the inflow from the etheric into biological/living matter to carry instructions for the pattern of a growing structure.

5. Who is capable of knowing the retained information?

Purusha, the Self, the pure Consciousness is the seer. What is seen? The whole of nature, beginning with the mind, down to gross matter.

In Chapter 3, Patanjali describes a capability called Samyama, which is the inclusive term for three progressive states of attention: concentration, meditation, and absorption (Samadhi). Various psychic powers (called siddhis) are acquired and manifested by directing Samyama on specific objects, thoughts, or phenomena. For example, Samyama on the navel chakra yields knowledge of the body's constitution; samyama on the spiritual heart (hrdaya), the centre of our being yields knowledge of the nature of consciousness[3]

---

[3] In this chapter, Patanjali enumerates several possibilities and potential powers such as moving through Akasha, clairvoyance, and clairaudience. He says that the yogi acquires mastery of Prakriti in other words, control of Nature.

(Trine 2010). Some individuals may be endowed with siddhis by birth. When someone is born with a siddhi, it is because of the samskaras that someone developed in a previous birth. In this birth he is born, as it were, to enjoy the fruits of them.

After reading the Yoga Sutras of Patanjali, Oliver found a description of Samadhi (Samapatti being one kind of Samadhi), in Yoga Sutra 1.41. He also found that one enters this state when all fluctuations of the mind are brought under control. Sutra 1.41 says the following: The Yogi whose Vrttis (thoughts) have become powerless (controlled) obtains in the receiver, receiving, and received (the self, the mind and objects of perception), concentration and sameness, like the crystal (before different coloured objects.) What results from this constant meditation? In a previous aphorism Patanjali went into the various states of meditation, and how the first will be the gross, and the second the fine objects, and from them the advance is to still finer objects of meditation. Here the Yogi sees the three things, the receiver, the received, and the receiving, corresponding to the soul, the object, and the mind. There are three objects of meditation given us. First, the gross things: bodies, or material objects, second, fine things: the mind, and third, the egoism. By practice, the Yogi gets established in all these meditations. Whenever he meditates he can keep out all other thought; he becomes identified with that which he mediates upon; when he meditates he is like a piece of crystal before flowers; the crystal becomes almost identified with flowers. If the flower is red, the crystal looks red, or if the flower is blue, the crystal looks blue. In chapter 3 of Yoga Sutras, it is said that it is only in the beyond-sensory perception of samadhi that we see an object in the truth of its own nature, absolutely free from the distortions of our imagination. Samadhi is, in fact, much more than perception; it is direct knowledge.

One of Oliver's Samapatti experiences which provides an example of the above scenario is as follows: He had been called to the hospital bedside of his daughter who was in a coma, having rejected an earlier heart and lungs transplant. As he sat looking at her he went into a state of intense bliss, hardly the response one would expect from a father looking at his dying daughter. As in other Samapatti examples mentioned earlier, by meditating upon the state of mind of his daughter, Oliver, the seer became aware of the state of his subject'/daughter's mind; the seer was also aware that the subject's mind was in that state but not Oliver's.

Oliver is sure that he experienced her state of mind by merging his mind with hers because Oliver never experienced the same bliss when he remembered and reported that event to others later in life. She must have been in a state of bliss at that time; she might have been in an NDE since NDEs usually have feelings of love, joy, peace, and/or bliss. Moreover, since one aspect of Samadhi is absence of grief, its absence in the above situation is another indication of being in the Samadhi state. We may say that in this Samapatti experience, while the seer is Purusha (Oliver being in the state of Purusha because he is the conscious being), the object of knowledge, the state of bliss of his daughter in coma is in Mahat.

Yoga Sutra 4.1 says that psychic powers may be obtained either by birth, or by means of drugs, or by the power of words (blessings from others), or by the practice of austerities, or by Samadhi. Hence Samadhi is not the only way to know information that survives the bodily death of an individual. As an example, clairvoyant, Claire Barry who is also an astrologer, palmist and numerologist wrote about life after death, meaning consciousness after death, in her book Godlet (Barry 2016). A client, we shall call him Steven, sought help from Claire in understanding events in his personal life, specifically, to find out if there was any spiritual method for proving one way or another whether those close to him had been associated with him at other times. By reading Steven's astrological chart she could say that indeed, some had been in similar relationships at another time and place. Steven flew to France to put Claire's astrological conclusions to test and began an odyssey covering the lives of this person and his extended family and acquaintances. Throughout Steven's journey, Claire gave him information about the culture, the landscape, and geography in such minute detail that he could find the exact place, and exact house he needed to reach.

6. Conclusion

"Does Consciousness End, Continue, Awaken, or Transform When the Body Dies?" is a question which, occupied the minds of prominent thinkers of all civilizations ever since ancient times. Interest in finding answers to this question continues even today as seen from the growing literature on reincarnation, NDEs, OBEs, and other paranormal phenomena. We have presented personal experiences of one of the authors (Oliver's), of a conscious but thoughtless state called Samapatti, as examples to support the view that consciousness is independent of the body. Oliver got into the Samapatti state whenever he focussed his mind on a human or animal subject; in that state, his mind became still and then he became aware of some physical or psychological conditions of the subject. Hence these experiences showed one can be conscious without the usual in-and-out thought flow and be aware of something external to one's own body and mind without any physical or sensory connection. Thus, they show that consciousness is not produced by the body or brain. If consciousness is independent of the body, it follows that consciousness does not end, nor awaken, nor transform with bodily death but continues unaffected.

According to Hindu Philosophy, consciousness (if interpreted as the ability to know) is not created by the body or brain and is always there everywhere unaffected by the birth, life, and death of any individual. This philosophy also says that the mind which is an accumulation of the information content of all conscious experiences in one's life together with any unconscious thoughts and desires, survives physical death as well; mind is not conscious by itself but it is the object of knowing, in other words, object of consciousness. Interestingly, today's research in NDE and OBE seems to validate Hindu philosophy's propositions that mind and consciousness are not necessarily dependent of the state of the body or brain. Many Eastern philosophies believe in the existence of a soul in each living being which does not end with the death of the body but can take another life; the soul may carry with it some of the surviving mind into the new life. Again, today's research in reincarnation seems to support Hindu philosophy's view that knowledge and influences of experiences in past lives may be carried over into a new life. The observation that some are able to report NDEs, OBEs, past-life experiences, etc. shows that the information content of such experiences must have been retained somewhere that is not a physical medium until its reporter is able to find it and report it, because the information is not known to others by normal (sensory and material) means. Patanjali yoga Sutras seem to have considered the question of where this information is stored.

7. Syamala Hari's References

Bailey Alice. The Light of the Soul: Its Science and Effect: a Paraphrase of the Yoga Sutras of Patanjali. Lucis, 1927.

http://www.thinkdownloads.com/download/Spiritual/Light%200P/020the%20Soul%20-%20Alice%20Bailey.pdf

Barry Claire. Godlet- From the Other Side of the Mirror. S.A. Design & Print. Port Elliot South Australia 5212. 2016.

Carr Bernard. Ian Stevenson and His Impact on Foreign Shores. Journal of Scientific Exploration 2008; 220): 87-92.

Greyson Bruce. Cosmological Implications of Near-Death Experiences. Journal of Cosmology, 2011; 14.

Hari S. How Vedanta Explains Conscious Subjective Experience. Journal of Consciousness Exploration & Research 2015; 6(4): 209 — 221.

Hari S, Oliver Alan J. Explaining Samapatti & Knowing without Mind by Vedanta. Journal of Consciousness Exploration & Research 2015; 6(12): 1001 -1014.

Hari S. Psychons could be zero-energy tachyons. Neuro Quantology. 2008, 6 (2): 152.

Hari S. Mind and Tachyons: How Tachyon Changes Quantum Potential and Brain Creates Mind. Neuro Quantology 2011, 9(2): 255.

Hari S. Mind and Tachyons: Quantum interactive dualism - Libet's causal anomalies. NeuroQuant010gy 2014, 12(2)•, 247.

Hari S. Mind and tachyons in six-dimensional special relativity. Neuro Quantology 2016, 14(1): 94-105.

Jacka Judy. The Human Energy Field. ACNEM Journal December 2011; 30 (3): 5.

Kihlstrom John F. The rediscovery of the unconscious. In H. Morowitz & J. L. Singer (Eds.). The mind, the brain, and complex adaptive systems. Addison-Wesley Publishing Co, Inc. 1994; 123-143. http://socrates.berkeley.edu/—kihlstrm/rediscovery.htm

Lingham. Durgadas (Rodney). Secrets of the Mahat: The Cosmic Intelligence. Lulu.com. 2013.

Mormann Florian and Koch Christof. Scholarpedia 2007; 2(12): 1740.

Mukherjee B D. The Essence of Bhagavad Gita. Academic Publishers 2002; Kolkata.

Smythies John R. Consciousness and Higher Dimensions of Space. Journal of Consciousness Studies 2012; 19(11-12): 224-232.

Stevenson Ian. Twenty Cases Suggestive of Reincarnation. University of Virginia Press, 1980. https://med.virginia.edu/perceptual-studies/

Swami Prabhvaananda and Christopher Isherwood. The Yoga Aphorisms of Patanjali. Sri Ramakrishna Math, Mylapore, Chennai, India. http://www.estudantedavedanta.net/YogaAphorisms-of-Patanjali.pdf

Swami Shravananda. Kenopanishad. The Ramakrishna Math, Mylapore, Madras 1920.

Swami Vivekananda. Raja Yoga. Kegan Paul, Trench Trubner & Company, Limited, 1893.

http://hinduonline.co/DigitalLibrary/SmallBooks/PatanjaliYogaSutraSwamiVivekanandaSanEng .pdf

Swami Vivekananda. The Vedanta Philosophy. The Vivekanada Foundation. http://web.csulb.edu/—wweinste/vedanta.html http://shardsofconsciousness.com/user/sites/shardsofconsciousness.com/files/ebooks/RajaYoga_ Vivekananda.pdf

Trine Cheryl. The New Akashic Records: Knowing, Healing& Spiritual Practice. Essenti

Another scholar I met through JCER was Meera Chakravorty, a Sanskrit expert from Bangalore, who also helped me understand my Samapatti. Meera Chakravorty wrote a book, Consciousness, Time, and Praxis[23], and through our discussions of her book, she was able to explain the wave/particle conundrum for me.

Meera recommended I read the Tarkasamgraha[26], a primer for Indian Logic. I read both books and I can see that wave/particle question relates to the same old chestnut, *i,* with the wave being the quantum information or manifestative cause, and the particle its manifested matter in a whole reality. Fig.6.1. on page 94, includes a line under the bottom of the yoga diagram to illustrate my notional interface between the unmanifested energy and its quantum potential active information, and the manifested matter.

I don't know whether the concept of imaginary numbers has any relationship to physicists' antimatter, but I can understand that, like Bohm and his wholeness, almost any physicist deeply focused on a problem could become close to the Siddhi state of realisation and needing to express his/her idea about a situation in which an unmanifested particle and its manifested partner are in a quantum entanglement (on the other side of zero), might find *i,* a convenient option.

Patanjali tells us that 'the knowing (knowledge) seeks to be known and is expressed in being.' The word, realise, means to give actual form and thus, to become real. Yoga Sutra 3. 17., says that "The sound, the meaning (behind it) and the idea (which is present in the mind at the time) are present together in a confused state. By performing Samyama (on the sound) they are resolved and there arises comprehension of the meaning of sounds uttered by any living being." When viewed as a quantum interaction, Contemplation or Meditation on the sound can resolve the confusion into their distinct explanations. It is likely that this conflation, seen from the 'normal mind perspective' is really that the three distinct contexts of the information in question are in an asymmetric relationship, perhaps I could go so far as to say it is Einstein's relativity on display.

All of this is related to Bohm's Wholeness and the Implicate Order, not just in what I have written, but in the interplay of the people I met along the way. Swami Veda Bharati mentions mystics and psychics as well as yogis, and I know two psychics in particular who have been of great benefit to Cecily and me; Monica Ward and Claire Barry, because they fill in some of the gaps in terms of the emotional intelligence present in the individual 'manifestative cause' we all must deal with in our life.

What the independence of consciousness tells us (if we care to know it at all), is that the source of all the pain and pleasure experienced in human life comes from the illusion that mind is authoritative and reliable. This is why an individual can think the mind is always right. The illusion is validated by what we can measure in brain activity, and that measurement becomes the validation of our physical and mental identity as a human being, and in the process it becomes a belief.

The problem with measurement of brain activity is that we are taking a physical measurement, which means we are measuring something between zero and the physical reality. This is a limit in terms of classical physics, and until the advent of quantum mechanics there was nothing beyond this limit.

To be fair, in considering the very small in a quantitative sense, physicists were aware of the radical changes in the accepted properties of matter when temperature for instance approached absolute zero. In the quantum considerations of matter below the level of atoms, and in a physical sense, this is a similar zero point, beyond which the nature of matter becomes very uncertain.

So, in terms of the consciousness of Ishvara, it is reasonable to say that the *consciousness* of Ishvara is independent of matter, and therefore, *it must be independent of mind.* If we apply that conclusion to Bohm and Hiley's 'active information' we can see how the 'will of God' applies in a practical sense, rather than in a human sense, and is independent of mind in the absolute sense.

The fact that this 'will of God' consciously applies the 'retained information' of Ishvara, rather than the will of an individual soul/ atman (based on the individual's experience), to the momentary quantum interaction, and it is this 'active information' that can produce an outcome. When that outcome is one the individual would have wished to avoid, we call that outcome 'karma.' This is possibly why humans conclude that God is judgemental when in fact, that is not true at all. God (or Ishvara) is impartial, dispassionate, and 'without distinguishing mark.'

The final point in the discussion of Consciousness being independent of the body is found in Patanjali's Yoga Sutras, Samadhi Pada, in the single word, advaita, which is listed in the glossary. The word translates as non-dual, and is accompanied by advaita-yoga, meaning the yoga of non-duality.

What this tells me is that Consciousness is not present in the living form; it enters the living form through the Samapatti of the Consciousness of Ishvara as the seer, and all living forms as the subject of that Samapatti relationship. As I have described in my Samapatti experiences, the subject is aware of the seer's consciousness while the seer is aware of the subject's consciousness. The significant point is that the seer is aware of both 'minds,' while the subject is only aware of the seer's observation in that moment, and for the subject, that awareness becomes a memory while for the seer it is just an observation, with 'no distinguishing mark.'

This overriding lack of a distinguishing mark is what makes Ishvara dispassionate, and in my opinion makes Consciousness dispassionate too. Moreover, this dispassionate aspect is the basis for my support of the term advaita, non-duality, being applied to Purusha, Brahma, God, Allah. It also means that the whole fundamental process operates at a level above Artificial Intelligence because it is Karma in its most loving and brutal form. For those who aspire to contact other life forms in the universe, be careful what you seek because they too will be conscious and operate through Karma. They could well be incarnations of you or me.

The other aspect of karma and the retention of information is the presence of radiation across the whole universe, commonly referred to as the Cosmic Microwave Background Radiation. From an independent/non-scientific viewpoint, I can only suggest that it covers a widespread spectrum of wavelengths. An example of this is the part of the spectrum visible to psychics, usually described as auras. If I had a scientific mind I would say that this partly visible radiation is also On The Other Side of Zero in that it is the fields of the Manifestative Cause in Einstein's MC^2, the forces which contribute to the solidity of the former potential that has become matter.

The forces in question are Gravity, Electromagnetism and the weak and strong nuclear forces, which have been 'created' out of 'nothing' to produce actual matter from unmanifested energy. I am suggesting that parts of the forces needed to manifest tangible matter, such as the Cosmic Microwave Background Radiation, remain after the collapse of a black hole, and that it is thinkable that gravity as a real force remains as well, which could account for the assumption of 'dark energy,' which may be what has been missing in the calculations of the matter which is the universe.

CHAPTER 10

This asymmetric 'walk-in' life

The Vedic position on the question of whose life? is that there is only one Self. For most people, this self is me, I am, the one in this body, and that last statement, 'the one in this body' is what defines us all because it is 'my mind.' What that statement, *the one in this body does*, is to assert Selfhood, and so it defines the mind as I am.

At birth, one is born without a name until the parent 'gives the infant' its name, and from the point forward the infant is taught who it *is*. And from birth is accumulates its own personal relationship with manifestative cause in spacetime. The infant's relationship with asymmetric spacetime, asymmetric memory, asymmetric Self, indeed, all things asymmetric, remain unknown and unpredictable through asymmetric karma.

If my 'walk-in moment' had occurred at the birth of 'this body,' my life would have followed a different path because the selfhood would have been lived in a familiar body from birth, but that wasn't the case. To understand how and why this happened I can only resort to the Siddhi state and ask my own questions. From my perspective, my life has been difficult at times as those around me left for reasons I didn't understand.

It is only now, in the closing years of this life, that I can ask these questions in terms of that universal asymmetry and wait to see what comes from that fountain of retained information. What I have been able to observe in retrospect is that my 'second birth' was probably on October 28, 1939, when I was four years old. I base that first assumption on the fact that most major changes in this 'second life' happened around that date. The most notable events being my first 'engagement to marry', my first marriage, the death of my last child, the end of my first marriage, and the death of my first child, all happened within the same day, in the same month, spaced across 60 something years.

In October of 2021, I moved from my home in South Australia to the state of Victoria to live with my daughter Kelly and I have spent most of my time since then writing Part 2 of "Thinking on the Other Side of Zero'. This final chapter is what has come to mind as I ask myself has there been a question I haven't asked?, and as usual, that is the question. "What was the point of this walk-in life?" I can only keep typing to find the answer as I think about the question.

From my present perspective, this life of Alan has been a classroom in which I have explored this 'walked-in state' and what it has to teach us about there being only one Self. Patanjali explains this by giving us the Yoga Sutras, in which there is only one conscious observer; Purusha, who is the seer in a Samapatti relationship with every living form.

From birth, an individual is taught to know her/his name and relationship to others in that family. In my case, I learned to be a member of a family and had an observed or unobserved Near-Death event in hospital. In that 'in between' moment of Near-Death Alan the individual 'died' as a result of the prolonged high temperature, but this 'other' mind entered his body.

In view of my established Samadhi state, my lifelong confusion was due, at least in part to the fact that Alan's body came with its inherited DNA signature and the assumed neural responses. My problem was realised by my family because my known neural responses were absent, and I was assumed to be somewhat mentally compromised. I accepted that family diagnosis because my family were my home teachers.

When I began school I was able to learn what I was taught and performed well enough to keep up with the rest of my class in every subject. In fact, I had done better at school than my older siblings and that may have been due to my quiet nature because most of my older siblings were regarded as relatively unmanageable. My immediate older brother, Jim, was having a difficult time because he was dyslexic and that was never addressed in the 1930's and forties. Later, he was demonstrably the brightest of all of us.

After all the older ones had left home I had to take on all the work of providing fire wood and other jobs around the house as the only male because my father had worked in a distant town. I sent a lot of time alone, and in what was a walking meditative state. I attended a Technical School and, like the other boys, expected to take up an apprenticeship. I wasn't impressed with what was available locally and joined the RAAF as a radio apprentice.

My RAAF service was unremarkable, as was my later civilian life, and spent a lot of my working life repairing things with little or no thought until my Samapatti experiences raised the questions I have been asking ever since. As I have written earlier, these questions were only part of the whole point of this other walk-in Alan; I can only give the answers from what Patanjali can tell me from the Yoga sutras.

The first point related to a 'walk-in' is that there are two ways one can enter the Siddhi/Samadhi state; the first way being a life of instruction from an accredited guru and meditation, the second is to have been 'born that way'. The second point is what Patanjali calls 'without the trauma of birth,' which I take to be a 'walk-in' situation because it really does avoid the trauma of birth.

During this period of my 'second birth' or rebirth, I haven't been involved in any remarkable event which has contributed to the whole of mankind in any significant manner, which would answer the question of 'why go to the bother of substituting a different Alan for the previous Alan in this body at a time of endemic poverty and stress?' I don't believe this is a more acceptable form of teaching people to achieve the Siddhi state; which leaves me with the answer of drawing attention to the fact of the Siddhi state as the consciousness of Purusha/Ishvara being the active information mentioned in Bohm's Wholeness and the Implicate Order rather than an individual's attainment of that state.

This is not to say that either form of attainment is better than the other. What the walk-in state provides us with, is an emphasis on the body-independence of Consciousness, and therefore, the Siddhi state asserts that the real Self is individual-independent. This is what I have learned from these two Alans, and for that I am grateful.

Alan Oliver

PART 2 REFERENCES:

1. Thinking on the Other Side of Zero. Part1. Alan Joseph Oliver. 2005.
2. Thinking on the Other Side of Zero. Part 2. Alan Joseph Oliver. 2022.
3. The Yoga Sutras of Patanjali, Swami Veda Bharati, Published by Himalayan Institute of Yoga Science and Philosophy of the USA. Honesdale, PA 18431.
4. The Sankhya Karika, GS Srinivasan. Online.
5. Wholeness and the Implicate Order. David Bohm. Routledge Keegan Paul, UK. 1984.
6. "A Free Fall into Unstructured Thinking," self-published by Fast Books. Sydney, Australia, 1993.
7. EST. Erhard Seminar Training. USA. 1980.
8. Thinkerman and the Accident of Knowing. Self-published by Fast Books. Sydney, Australia. 1999.
9. The Fetzer Memorial Trust film, *Infinite Potential: The Life & Ideas of David Bohm[3].*"
10. The Science of Yoga. I.K. Taimni, Quest Books, Theosophical Publishing House. P.O. Box 270,Wheaton Ill. USA.
11. Geons, Black Holes, and Quantum Foam: A life in Physics John Archibald Wheeler & Kenneth Ford. 2010.
12. The Quantum Labyrinth. Paul Halpern. Basic Books. 2017.
13. Jesus The Man. Barbara Thiering. Corgi edition, 1993. London. UK.
14. The Book That Jesus Wrote. Barbara Thiering. Corgi edition, 1998 London UK.

15. The Guide for the Perplexed. Moses Maimonides, 12th century thinker.

16. The Arctic Home in the Vedas. Lokamanya Bal Gangadhar Tilak. Kindle edition.

17. Paradise Found: The Cradle of the Human Race at the North Pole. William Warren. 1880.

18. Thought as a System. David Bohm. Routledge. London.UK. 1992.

19. The Hard Problem of Consciousness. David Chalmers. online.

20. Stephen Hawking's Information Paradox. online.

21. The Undivided Universe. Bohm and Hiley. Routledge. London. 1993.

22. Body-Independence of Consciousness and Retained Information. Alan J Oliver and Syamala Hari. PhD.

23. Consciousness, Time, and Praxis. Meera Chakravorty. New Bharatiya Book Corporation. Delhi, India. 2007.

24. GODLET. From the Other Side of the mirror. Claire Barry.

25. NewScientist on March 19, 2005, p33.

26. Tarkasamgraha. A Primer of Indian Logic. Chowkhamba Vidyabhawan. Varanasi. India.

BODY-INDEPENDENCE OF CONSCIOUSNESS AND RETAINED INFORMATION

Alan J Oliver

thinkerman1@dodo.com.au

and

Syamala D Hari[4]

murty_hari@yahoo.com

ABSTRACT

In ancient times, Hindu philosophy thoroughly analysed consciousness, mind, body, and their relations to one another. The philosophy asserts that consciousness is independent of both body and mind, where mind means the accumulation of experiences, desires, aversion, emotions, etc. of a living being. Hence it asserts that consciousness does not end, nor awaken, nor transform with bodily death but continues unaffected. According to this philosophy, mind is not conscious just like lifeless matter but mind can interact with matter in suitable conditions. The theory of mind-brain interactions in Hindu philosophy may be called interactive dualism but it is NOT Cartesian dualism. We present experiences of one of the authors (Oliver's), of a conscious but thoughtless state called Samapatti, as examples to support the view that consciousness is not produced by the body. Oliver got into the Samapatti state whenever he focussed his mind on a human or animal subject; in that state,

---

4   Author for correspondence.

his mind became still and then he became aware of some physical or psychological conditions of his subject. These experiences show that one can be conscious without the usual in-and-out thought flow and be aware of something external to one's own body and mind without any physical or sensory connection. We point out that these apparently 'anomalous', experiences are possible realities described in the traditional sources of Hindu Philosophy. Since the topic of consciousness inevitably includes what one is conscious or aware of, we also discussed whether the information content of experiences accumulated during the life of a living being disappears after death, or whether at least some of it remains. Interestingly, today's researches in near-death experiences and reincarnation seem to validate Hindu philosophy's propositions that consciousness is not produced by the body or brain and that some mental contents survive bodily death (as implied by the so called principle of reincarnation).

Key words: Consciousness, Body and Mind, Samadhi, Samapatti, Bhagavad Gita, Yoga Sutras of Patanjali, Reincarnation, Near Death Experiences.

1. Introduction

The question, "Does consciousness end, continue, awaken, or transform when the body dies?" is one that occupied the minds of prominent thinkers of all civilizations ever since ancient times. Interest in finding answers to this question continues even today as seen from the growing literature on reincarnation, near-death experiences (NDEs), out-of-body-experiences (OBEs), and other paranormal phenomena. To answer the above question in its various aspects the authors have turned to personal experiences in the Samadhi and Samapatti states and to explanations from the Hindu traditional philosophies in Bhagavad Gita and the Yoga

Sutras of Patanjali, because these sources analysed relations among consciousness, mind, and body thoroughly. Interestingly, today's researches in NDEs, OBEs, and reincarnation seem to validate Hindu philosophy's propositions that consciousness is not produced by the body or brain and that some mental contents survive bodily death (as implied by the so called principle of reincarnation).

Phenomenal information (PI), the content of a conscious experience: In our lives, we have many conscious experiences. In any such experience, there is awareness of something, which may be an emotion, a desire, a thought etc., or awareness of seeing, hearing, touching, tasting, or smelling an external object accessed by one's senses. We may call this something information. There seems to be a subject, which we report as 'I' and there is ability to be aware, which seems to be available when we are awake but not in deep sleep; in dream sleep, there is ability to be aware of some imaginations but not of the sensory contacts with the outside world. Hence a conscious experience has three components to it: 1) the 'I', 2) some 'phenomenal information' (why we add the qualifier, 'phenomenal' will be explained in the following paragraphs), and 3) the act of knowing or being aware.

In the case of a sensory experience, for example, seeing an apple, this information is different from both the apple and its biological/ neural map created in the brain/body of the human (living) being. It is useful to note this difference because according to modern neuroscience, every subjective (conscious) state such as a conscious intention or conscious emotion, or perception of an external object, occurs only if a required and correlated neural process takes place. Each conscious state has its associated neural correlates of consciousness: one for seeing a red patch, another one for seeing grandmother, yet a third one for hearing a siren, etc. (Mormann and Koch 2007). Interestingly, one is never aware of the existence of the neural correlate (NC) in one's own brain. One is only aware of the NC's 'meaning', which must have been created along with the NC. In contrast, a neuroscientist monitoring the brain can see an image of the NC on the monitor but does not directly know the NC's 'meaning' (namely, what the owner of the brain is aware of). The neuroscientist will have to accept whatever the brain's owner reports as his/her experience.

Phenomenal information is different from matter. We (human beings) can report our conscious experiences to others, if we wish to do so. When we do, we use a language and any of several means: sounds, electrical signals, write on a paper, and so on. Every means of communication requires human (living) beings to ASSIGN meaning or information that is in our heads (which we called PI), to structures of matter or material energy. These structures carry a mapping of the PI; the structures themselves are not identical with the PI[5]. Yet, in our daily lives, we do not distinguish between PI and the means we use to communicate or store it outside our heads. For example, we say "the book has good information about the city", whereas the book only has words whose meanings exist in our heads but not in the book. Hence modern scientists called the information, which a living being is aware of in an experience 'phenomenal information' to emphasize that it is different from the language or energy signals

---

[5]   To begin with, a word in any language is not identical with its meaning because the same meaning may be conveyed by different words in different languages. A language is a mapping of PI into words (symbols) which become sound energy when pronounced, particles of matter when written on paper, and become electrical energy when transmitted over a telephone line, and so on.

used for its storage and communication or the corresponding neural/ biological activity in the body.

Fortunately for us, no means of communication, or information storage device, or a computer ever creates or assigns any new PI overwriting what we intended it to carry! Hence, we may assume that lifeless matter does not create PI all by itself. On the other hand, as long as we are awake, we experience more and more, thereby keep on accumulating more PI in our memory and this memory has two components: biological and mental. The mental component consists of PI; the biological component is what a monitoring instrument can convey physically/scientifically. We have to infer that the living matter in brain/body not only creates a biophysical map of a material object accessed by its senses but also creates a 'meaning' of the map, i.e., the associated PI.

PI is subjective. It is every day experience that one's thoughts cannot be seen, heard, etc., by others, i.e., by their senses, nor can they be accessed by any material instruments; one's thoughts are not known to others unless one conveys them verbally or by other physical means (making it very tempting to lie!). We call this inaccessibility of the mind by senses and material devices subjectivity[6].

PI is different from consciousness. One may ask "are phenomenal information (PI) and the ability to know different, or is consciousness a property of the former?" Many Western philosophers (for example, Descartes) do not see a distinction between the mind and consciousness whereas in Hindu and Buddhist philosophies, mind (an accumulation of PI) is said to be not conscious just like lifeless

---

[6]   In the following sections, we will describe how Hindu philosophy's dualistic theory of mind-body interactions explains why mind is not accessible to senses.

matter and to be different from consciousness! However even in the West, Leibniz, Helmholtz, Kant, and psychologists including William James, Sigmund Freud, and many others discussed existence of unconscious thought at length (Kihlstrom 1994). More recently, modern psychologists found evidence for unconscious thought and unconscious cognition[7]. Hence, we may assume that PI and the ability to know are different, and that consciousness is not a property of PI.

Now, from the point of view of physics, the body of a living being is made of the same fundamental particles of which lifeless matter is made. While lifeless matter outside any living body does not seem to create PI, every human body seems to be creating more and more experiences and accumulating PI in the wakeful and dream states. Since we all know that living matter inevitably becomes lifeless some time or other, the questions, "what happens to the PI accumulated until death and what happens to consciousness, i.e., the ability to know, which was there until death?" naturally arise. Answers to these questions are clearly very difficult to address by scientific means because both PI and consciousness are subjective. Some scientists simply assume that matter exists in two kinds of states: one living and the other lifeless, and that PI and consciousness are properties of living matter and therefore those properties disappear with change of state by death. Yet, since it is only an assumption so far but not yet proved by any scientific means, the possibility that consciousness

---

[7] Unconscious cognition is the processing of perception, memory, learning, thought, and language without being aware of it. The role of the unconscious mind on decision making is a topic greatly debated by neuroscientists, linguists and psychologists around the world. (https://en.wikipedia.org/wiki/Unconscious_cognition).

and/or some or all of the PI accumulated during life survive/s death does exist.

To explore that possibility in its various aspects, in this article, we turn to personal experiences in the Samadhi and Samapatti states described in traditional sources of Hindu philosophies such as Bhagavadgita and Yoga Sutras of Patanjali. We also cite some experiments of Bevan Reid, a distinguished medical scientist, who seemed to have found evidence of an etheric field in his laboratory space which could retain some "experiences" of living cells even after their death. We also point out that some prominent modern researchers of reincarnation, NDE, and OBE seem to agree with Hindu philosophy's principle of reincarnation and the view that consciousness is not produced by the body or brain.

2. Does Consciousness End, or Continue, When the Body Dies?

Hindu philosophy's answer to the above question is that consciousness continues unaffected; it is universal and fundamental and not altered by the death of an individual's body. A very brief summary of some of the teachings in Bhagavad Gita is as follows:

- There exists Universal Consciousness which is omnipresent, omniscient, and omnipotent.
- Every living being is associated with its own soul (*Jiva*) which is a part of that infinite Consciousness, who draws to itself the senses and the mind that are part of Nature (Bhagavad Gita Chapter 15, verse 7). Being part of the eternal Consciousness, the soul is eternal also and survives the death of the physical body.
- The Self (*Atman*) is Consciousness seated in the hearts of all beings (Bhagavad Gita chapter 10, verse 20).

- Kenopanishad (Swami, 1920) says that the mind and senses are able to perform their respective functions willed and supported by Consciousness; without Consciousness, the senses and the mind cannot function.
- The mind consists of ego (*ahamkara*), ability to think (*manas*), desires, aversion, emotions, experiences, etc. (*chitta*), and intellect (buddhi) which includes the ability to make decisions based on memory.
- Bhagavadgita describes the distinctions between the body mind complex and the one who 'knows' them (*shetrajna*). The Field (*shetra*) consists of the body, the senses and sense objects, the body's environment (Nature), and the mind. Nature includes the five elements: earth, water, fire, air and the sky, and the five senses: hearing, touching, seeing, tasting and smelling; objects of the senses are sound, touch, form and color, taste and smell.
- All contents of the Field, namely, the body, its environment, and the mind are said to be insentient (Bhagavad Gita, 7:4).
- The knower of the Field (*shetrajna*) is Consciousness Himself and His infinitesimal projection, *Jiva* who assumed this function within this body. As to the interaction of the body and the mind, in the chapter called *Karma Yoga*, Gita says that the senses influence the body, and *manas* and *chitta* influence the senses; *buddhi* influences the *manas* and *chitta*, and *Jiva* influences buddhi.
- The senses and the mind cannot grasp Consciousness, and no scientific theory can logically prove His existence (Kenopanishad), and therefore no scientific experiments can detect Him either. The same thing is true about *Jiva*.

Individual consciousness perceived in living beings differs from Universal Consciousness (we call this Consciousness with a big C in front) in that the former is fragmented. An individual's consciousness exists only in wakeful and dreaming sleep states and knows only one thing at a time and in general, one individual usually does not know the conscious experience of another whereas Universal consciousness knows everything everywhere all the time! It is explained in Hindu philosophy why each individual mind appears to be conscious. It is because the Universal Consciousness creates a reflection (*pratibimba*) as it were, in each mind and this reflection is the 'I' thought called *ahamkara* in Sanskrit and appears to be conscious; it is the individual consciousness.

Mind is faster than matter – Subjectivity of mind: Some Hindu philosophers may say that mind is subtle matter. This statement is an abridgement of the following: that mind is not accessible to senses, that it is as insentient as lifeless matter, and that the body and the mind interact with, and influence each other throughout life. The statement should not be understood to mean that mind is the same as, or a state of the physical matter, which sciences such as physics and chemistry have studied so far. Modern science deals with matter which is accessible to senses directly or indirectly via material instruments. By asserting mind's inaccessibility to senses, Hindu philosophy posits mind as different from gross physical matter or even material energy; for example, the so called principle of reincarnation depends upon the proposition that some mental contents called *vasanas* or *samskaras* survive bodily death.

In Hindu philosophy, 'mind control' is a major topic. It is often said that one who can keep the mind free of all thoughts can see for oneself the true nature[8] of consciousness. Controlling the mind is recognized as a difficult task and various techniques are prescribed to 'control' the mind. It is emphasized that the mind is restless and cannot come to a stop (it is a common experience that thoughts keep rising one after another when one is awake or in the dream state). The mind is described as being very fast, faster than the senses, faster than physical matter and material energy, and faster than anything in the physical world, in other words, faster than light. It is our everyday experience that our minds are subjective. Clearly, Hindu philosophy explains why mind is subjective; the energy which physical senses can grasp is limited by the speed of light and therefore senses cannot grasp something that is faster than light.

Interestingly, assuming the theme that mind is faster than matter, mind brain interactions can be described as tachyon interaction with ordinary non-relativistic matter. This mathematical model of mind-brain interaction is interactive dualism and shows how the brain creates PI (subjective experience) if the mind pays attention to the brain (Hari 2011). This model also explains why every subjective experience (including remembering a past experience) happens 'now' in one's mind (Hari 2016). This model was successful in explaining and justifying Eccles's hypothesis about the role of volition in

---

[8]   Consciousness or *Atma* when it is joined to nature, appears to feel either pleasure or pain. Whenever an event or object is perceived a thought-wave (*vritti*) raises in the mind. *Ahamkara*, the ego-sense identifies itself with this wave. This false identification is the cause of all our misery. One cannot recognize one's real Self as long as this false identification exists. An analogy explains this. If the water in a lake is muddy or is agitated, the bottom cannot be seen. If the water is clear, and there are no waves, we see the bottom. So with the mind; when it is calm, we see what our own nature is; we do not mix our self but remain our own selves. Hence Hindu philosophy teaches many techniques to bring the mind to stillness.

exocytosis, the basic process of inter-neuronal communication (Hari 2008), and Libet's causal anomalies (Hari 2014).

Living being – computer analogy: Descriptions of Consciousness, mind, and body and their relations summarized above may be better understood using the following analogy: The physical body of a living being is like a piece of hardware. It is made up of matter. Every living being, human or animal, or any living organism (possibly excluding some primitive forms of life), has an accumulation of experiences, desires, aversion, emotions, etc., and therefore an accumulation of information, in other words a memory, which we is called mind in this paper. In this sense, mind is like a computer memory containing data and programs. Just like a computer's hardware and software do not know what they are doing, their own existence, and the meaning of their memory contents, both the body and the mind of a living being also do not really know anything but there is a certain Consciousness (apart from the mind mentioned above) that "knows". Consciousness is like the computer operator, as it were, and the one who "really knows" everything that is part of the living being's activity. The ability to think (logical reasoning), and the ability to make decisions based on existing contents are similar to computer programs in that they can exist in an active or a passive state. They create new PI (what one is aware of in a new experience) by being active; after new PI is created they remain in the memory in a passive state until they are called upon for action again.

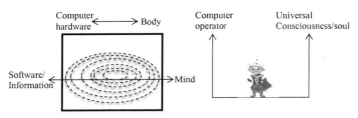

The mind and the body are both not conscious just like the hardware and software of a computer. Only Consciousness and soul really know and have control over all that happens in an individual's life. Mind is subtle and its magic is visible only when it is working with the body similar to the way the capabilities of software (also subtle) are visible only when it is loaded into the computer and activated.

Figure 1. Computer analogy of Consciousness, Mind, and Body Relations in Vedanta

Oliver's Samapatti seems to indicate that consciousness is independent of the body and the mind. Samapatti is a conscious state, where there are no thoughts flowing in and out. In the Patanjali's Yoga tradition[9], Samapatti would be classified as a Siddhi, a capability gained through the application of Samadhi, a state of consciousness which is attained through meditation and which lies beyond waking, dreaming, or deep sleep. Samadhi may be attained by single-pointed concentration that slows down mental activity to a complete stop. When Oliver focused his mind on a human or animal subject, he entered the Samapatti state and became aware of some physical and psychological conditions of the subject. All his subjects experienced peace as their anxieties gradually cleared during the session. In that state, Oliver could see and know beyond our normal experience of seeing and knowing; he did not need a physical connection to the subject to know the subject's state of mind. After reading the Yoga

---

[9] Oliver's quest for understanding his own experiences led him to a branch of the Hindu philosophy because most Western philosophies do not see a distinction between thought and consciousness whereas in Hindu and Buddhist philosophies, the mind is said to be not conscious just like lifeless matter.

Sutras of Patanjali he found a description of Samadhi, in Yoga Sutra 1.41 and that his state of mind in his healing sessions would be called Samapatti (one kind of Samadhi) according to the Sutras. Let us now recall some of Oliver's Samapatti experiences as a healer (Oliver 2010). In a later section, we will see that they match the description of Samadhi by the Yoga Sutras.

In one instance, Oliver's subject was a disturbed cat which was antisocial and hadn't washed itself for more than a year. As he focused on it with closed eyes, his mind became still. He became aware that the cat went to sleep and had chaotic visual images, a bit like multiple auras of migraine. He then felt that the chaos cleared to become a garden scene viewed from cat eye-level, with very large plants and shades of brown, yellow and red colors. At the same time, he was also aware that he had never seen the garden before and that the images were not in his own mind but that he watched the cat's dream. After a while, when Oliver felt that the cat would wake up, it woke up and began to wash itself suggesting that the disturbances in its mind subsided during the Samapatti session. In another instance, Oliver fixed his mind on the fractured leg of a lady waiting for a bone graft. Once again his mind attained stillness and he became aware of the physical distress within the bone. He silently wished to replace the distress which he felt was dark, with something bright and vibrant like gold. When he opened his eyes, she told him with excitement that she visualized bright gold energy replacing some black stuff in the bone. A week later, she had the leg x-rayed in preparation for a bone graft; the x-ray showed new bone growth at the fracture site. There is an interesting point here: Normally (if not in Sampatti), Oliver is unable to visualize anything. That the lady visualized the wish of Oliver while he was in Sampatti, and reported the visualization to him after the session, confirmed to him that in the case of the session with the cat, the garden scene was the dream of the cat and not his visualization or hallucination.

One common aspect of all Sampatti experiences of Oliver is that while he was in the state of stillness, those anxieties, disturbances, perturbations, etc., that were there earlier in his subject's mind gradually cleared and the subject's mind also became still. For instance, he worked over some years with a lady called Emma, who had breast cancer and helped her to come to terms with whatever the outcome might be. Samapatti sessions were her favourites because when he went into stillness her pain and her concern for herself stopped as she too became still and thereby peaceful. Another person who suffered from Huntington's chorea was helped by Oliver using Samapatti. His uncontrollable movements ceased for the duration of the session, typically around 45 minutes. Since the random movements ceased while he was asleep, as is the nature of the disease, obviously during the Sampatti session this person's mind and brain also calmed down similar enough to mimic sleep, although he was awake.

In all his Samapatti sessions, Oliver was aware of his own state of mind as well as that of his subject's, and was able to know which was his own and which was the subject's. The explanation from Hindu philosophy for this experience is as follows (Hari and Oliver 2015): once the seer disconnects his/her identification with his/her body by focusing on the subject, he/she is in the thoughtless state with no *ahamkara* and raises to the level of Consciousness in Figure 1, the operator of all computers. Just as a computer operator can see the contents of two computers, Consciousness can see the memory contents of both individuals, the seer and the subject, and know that anxiety is in the subject's memory but not in the seer's memory. Again like the computer operator, Consciousness can enter this fact into the seer's memory; Consciousness could also remove anxious thoughts and hyperactivity in the subject's minds and make them peaceful during the session. Ordinary living beings who cannot break their identification with the body and mind cannot exchange their memory contents without using senses just like computers cannot communicate without a material connection. The common aspects of Oliver's Sampatti sessions and the sequence of events in a typical session are presented pictorially in Figure 2.

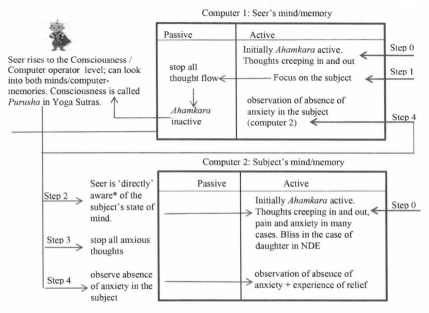

* Seer is like a piece of crystal before flowers; the crystal becomes almost identified with flowers. If the flower is red, the crystal looks red, or if the flower is blue, the crystal looks blue. It is the beyond-sensory perception of *samadhi* that grasps the true nature of an object in reality, absolutely free from the distortions of our imagination. *Samadhi* is, in fact, much more than perception; it is direct knowledge.

Figure 2. A pictorial representation of sequence of events in Samapatti

Experiences such as above show that one can remain conscious although the usual thought flow in one's mind has stopped. They also show that one (the seer) could know another's mind without requiring a physical connection, which ability is beyond our normal knowing experience. They make one wonder whether real Consciousness is distinct from what we usually see and call consciousness in living beings. These seemingly impossible events suggest that Consciousness must be something quite distinct from the brain and its memory/PI. If one's ability to know is independent of one's brain, it would follow that the ability does not cease to exist when the body dies.

Near-Death Experiences (NDE) indicate that consciousness and mind exist independently of the body. Nowadays, there is growing interest among scientists in NDE research as they hear reports from hospitals that patients who have been declared clinically dead exhibited various mental capabilities such as cognition, perception, and memory with enhanced mental clarity under cerebral impairment conditions such as cardiac arrest and general anaesthesia, when such mental activity cannot be associated with normal brain function. An example of enhanced mental functioning during an NDE is a rapid revival with exceptional clarity of memories that extends over the person's entire life. Researchers call one type of experience as veridical NDE, in which experiencers acquire verifiable information that they could not have obtained by any normal means. For example, some experiencers reported seeing events going on at some distant location, such as another room of the hospital while they are unconscious. Some reported visions of deceased persons, including those not previously known to be deceased, and it was found later that the demises had actually happened.

A common feature of near-death or after death experiences is the remarkable clarity of their reports surpassing those of normal waking state. In some NDE, the experiencers even acquired information which they could not have obtained by any normal means but which was indeed verified to be true later on. Greyson (2011) argues that if the mind is solely dependent on the brain for its existence, clarity of mental activity should be diminishing in clinical death conditions, and knowledge of events without the required sensory inputs would be impossible. In his view, these features of NDEs indicate that mind may only be dependent on the brain much as a radio transmission is dependent upon a receiver and broadcast unit but mind is not dependent on the brain to the extent that it cannot exist or function when the brain cannot function. Greyson thinks that the observed correlation between brain states and mind states is compatible with the theory that mind is produced by the brain, but it is also compatible with the theory that the brain may be a vehicle which receives, transports, and transmits, but is not synonymous with the mind.

Greyson's view of the brain-mind relationship is compatible with our view of it, namely, that the relation is similar to the hardware-software relationship in a computer (Hari 2015). We think that the brain plays the role of hardware and the mind plays the role of the software in creating new experience/information. Information stored in a computer is of two kinds: data and programs. The former are passive. Any program is of the latter kind; it is passive until it is activated. Once activated, the program runs and creates outputs which are new records/information in the memory. To do even the simple task of creating a record of any input, the computer needs to have a "WRITE" instruction, a program, already in its memory. The input activates the stored program, which then runs in the hardware (i.e., the hardware goes through a dynamic process) and creates passive records. After the activity is over, the program goes back to its passive state. The point to note is that hardware does not produce new records all by itself; it takes both hardware and software to do so. Similarly, to produce a new experience, a thinking activity, which is an interaction of already existing thoughts with the biological matter, needs to take place in the brain. New mental records are produced as a result of the process. The activity may be initiated by a desire/purpose (thoughts), or by sensory inputs, the soul or by Consciousness. Similar to a computer program, at the end of a thinking activity which involves both body and mind, those mental contents which participated in the activity still remain passively in the memory[10]. Again, the main point to note here is that the brain does not create new information all by itself; it needs to interact with already stored information/mind to produce the new information. Like hardware and software in a computer, brain and mind are not identical. The brain serves as the receiver of sensory inputs for creating sensory experience and as the broadcast unit for communicating its mind (stored information) to others.

Thus, like Samapatti experiences, NDEs also indicate that both consciousness and mind exist independent of the body and therefore suggest the possibility of their survival after bodily death.

3. Does the information accumulated until death survive death? – Reincarnation

Having noted that the mind/PI of a brain is different from the brain although the brain plays a role in creating the PI, one may ask what happens to the PI accumulated until death. Hindu philosophy's answer to this question is that the accumulated information remains after death.

The theory of mind-brain interactions in Hindu philosophy may be called interactive dualism because while recognizing both mind's

---

[10]   For example, a violinist has the ability to play violin but he/she does not play violin all the time. The ability to play violin is stored in the musician's memory in a passive state and he/she activates it to perform. He/she enjoys the music while playing violin and remembers the experience even afterwards. After the performance is done, the ability to play violin is still there and no one else knows about the musician's talent unless he/she performs.

action upon the body and the body/brain's role in creating experience, mind is considered neither as a state of the biological matter in the body nor as an emergent property of it but. The contents of mind are said to be faster than matter and light implying that they are different from organic or inorganic matter. In fact, the basis for the well-known principle of reincarnation is that some mental contents called *vasanas* or *samskaras* survive bodily death. However, this theory is NOT Cartesian Dualism because the philosophy affirms the existence of a supreme Consciousness and an individual *Jiva* who are immaterial; they are beyond the mind. The ego (the I-feeling called *ahamkara*) is part of the mind and not conscious. Hence neither Jiva nor the ego is the 'I' of Descartes who presumes that the mind, the 'I', and soul are more or less the same thing and that it is conscious.

In Hindu philosophy, life is the process of interaction between the body and the mind (in the computer analogy, this interaction is similar to execution of software in the hardware). Life begins when mind starts interacting with the body and lasts as long as the interaction continues. At death, the body is no longer able to support the interaction (just like a computer with defective hardware does not support software execution). Further, the philosophy proposes that some accumulated latent impressions of all past experiences, and desires called *vasanas* or *samskaras* survive the death of the physical body and carried by the immortal *Jiva* into a new life[11] if the *Jiva* is not yet detached from them and therefore not liberated but bound to experience consequences of actions in previous lives. The new life gives *vasanas* another chance for expression. This is the principle of

---

[11] In Aphorism 2.9, Patanjali says that the desire to cling to life is inherent both in the ignorant and in the learned. This is because the mind retains impressions of the death experience from many previous incarnations; after all, how could we fear death so much if we had never previously experienced it?

reincarnation believed in Hindu and other Eastern philosophies and religions and not found in Western philosophies and religions. This principle does not appear too unreasonable because it is similar to the following scenario involving a computer's software and hardware: a computer with broken hardware cannot run a piece of software which if saved on a storage device, can be entered into another computer and made to run again!

Today, reincarnation is the subject of recent investigations by many parapsychologists, psychics, and even psychiatrists. Belief in the reality of reincarnation is gaining support even from scientists such as Carr (a physicist) and Smythies (a neuroscientist). One of the noteworthy researches on this topic is by Stevenson, who was a Professor of Psychiatry and Director or the Division of Perceptual Studies at the University of Virginia. He compiled and studied voluminous data that appear to provide scientific proof that reincarnation is real. In one of his books (Stevenson 1967), he shows by scientific reasoning why reincarnation is the only viable explanation that fits the facts of his study. He was able to rule out alternative explanations for his twenty cases of young children who were spontaneously able to describe events in a previous life as soon as they learned to talk. His study is also reproducible by any sceptic so that doubts about the validity of his study can be eliminated. Stevenson's later research further supported the reality of reincarnation because he travelled to the scenes reported in past-life accounts and interviewed witnesses to assess details provided in the accounts. In over 1000 of these cases, the past lives of these children could be factually validated.

If information about past lives is remembered by someone then in the time interval between any two of that someone's lives, the information must exist somewhere and not be destroyed. Where it is stored must be a non-physical medium because in that interval, it is not accessible to other living beings with normal sensory capabilities.

4. Where the information surviving death is retained

We said mind is a store of PI. During life, one's mind is obviously intimately linked with one's body because any ailments or impairments of the body are necessarily accompanied by corresponding defects in one's memory and ability to experience. So, once the body dies and is no longer able to report any piece of information, the assumption that information is not destroyed but remains, raises the question "where is the surviving information retained?" Patanjali's Yoga Sutras seem to have an answer for this question. The Sutras also say who is able to find/read/know that retained information.

Figure 3 illustrates cosmology according to the *Sankhya* philosophy which is part of the Yoga Philosophy. Samkhya states that the whole universe evolves from two sources: consciousness, or *Purusha,* the eternal reality, the real Self, *Atman* in Sanskrit; and nature, or *Prakriti,* pure creative power. Within *Prakriti* are the three fundamental forces: *tamas,* inertia and ignorance; *rajas,* momentum and desire; and *sattva,* balance, luminosity, and knowledge. They make up the *Prakriti* and are important principally as physio-psychological factors. The first stage of evolution from undifferentiated *Prakriti* is called Mahat, "the great cause" occurs when *Prakriti* is illuminated by the spiritual light of a *Purusha.* Mahat is universal intelligence, and each human mind is a part of that cosmic intelligence. From *Mahat* evolves individual *buddhi,* the discriminating faculty. From *buddhi* evolves *ahamkara,* the individual ego-sense. From *ahamkara,* the lines of evolution branch off in three different directions—to produce *manas,* the recording faculty; the five powers of perception (sight, smell, hearing, taste and touch); the five organs of action (tongue, feet, hands and the organs of evacuation and procreation); and the five *tanmatras*, which are the subtle inner essences of sound, feelings, aspect, flavor and odour. These subtle *tanmatras*, combining and recombining, are then said to produce the five gross elements of which the external universe is composed: earth, water, fire, air or gas including breath and *Prana*, and space (*Akasha*).

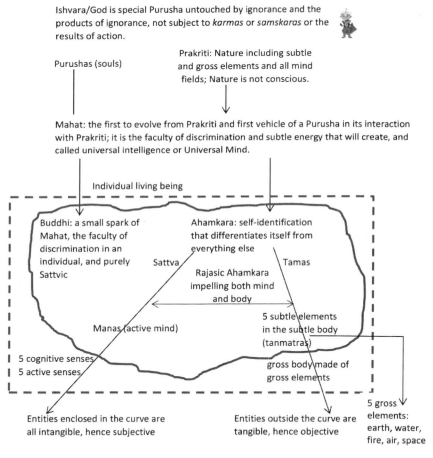

Figure 3. The Yoga perspective of creation

Purushas or souls are infinite in number and similar but separate, none superior to any other. *Purusha* is not the doer but the witness.

Experience is explained on the basis of a certain association of *Purusha* with nature. Nature is merely the medium for *Purusha* to manifest itself; Nature is not the source of consciousness. The mind seems to be intelligent and conscious whereas it has only a borrowed intelligence. Knowledge or perception is a thought-wave *(vritti)* in the mind. Since the mind is not the seer, but only an instrument of knowledge, it is also an object of perception like the outside world. The *Atman* is the real seer. Thus, to summarize, creation is described as an evolution outward, from undifferentiated into differentiated consciousness, from cosmic mind into universe. Pure consciousness is, as it were, gradually covered by successive layers of ignorance and differentiation, each layer being grosser and thicker than the one below it, until the process ends on the outer physical surface of the visible and tangible world (Swami Prabhvaananda).

False identification, right knowledge or Self-Realization: *Purusha*, when it is joined to nature, appears to feel either pleasure or pain. When an event or object is perceived, a thought-wave raises in the mind. *Ahamkara*, the ego-sense identifies itself with this wave. This false identification is the cause of all our misery; even the ego's temporary sensation of happiness brings anxiety, a desire to cling to the object of pleasure, and this prepares future possibilities of becoming unhappy. Although *Atman* remains forever outside the power of thought-waves, one can never know one's real Self as long as thought-waves and the ego-sense are being identified. To explain this, the commentators employ a simple analogy. If the water in a lake is muddy, the bottom will not be seen, or it is agitated all the time, the bottom will not be seen. If the water is clear, and there are no waves, we shall see the bottom. So with the mind; when it is calm, we see what our own nature is; we do not mix our self but remain our own selves. Hence Patanjali speaks of techniques of "control of thought-waves" at length[12].

Hindu philosophy believes in cycles of creation. The whole universe is composed of two materials, *Akasha* and *Prana*. *Akasha* is the omnipresent, all-penetrating existence. Everything that has form is evolved out of this *Akasha*. All force, whether gravitation, attraction or repulsion, or life, is the outcome of one primal force called *Prana*. *Prana* acting on *Akasha* creates or projects the universe. At the beginning of a cycle, there is only this *Akasha* and it is motionless and unmanifested. Then *Prana* begins to act, more and more, creating

---

[12]　Pursuing the analogy of the lake (Swami Prabhvaananda), let us consider banks of sand or pebbles built by waves by their continued action, at the lake bottom. They are, much more permanent and solid than the waves themselves. They may be compared to the tendencies, potentialities and latent states which exist in the subconscious and unconscious areas of the mind. They are called *samskaras*. *Samskaras* are built up by the continued action of thought-waves, and drive our actions. Another name for the carried over experience of an individual soul is Karma. A mental or physical act is called karma. *Karma* is also used to describe the consequence of an act, and hence to describe the sum of the consequences of our past actions in this and previous lives. Since *samskaras* drive actions and actions in their turn, produce new thought-waves, *samskaras* and Karma form an endless cycle. Yoga philosophy teaches us that it is the *samskaras* that drive us from birth to birth just as a strongly rooted addiction drives a man to take a drug, over and over again.

Purusha who is in the state of ignorance by mistakenly identifying itself with aspects of *Prakriti* is equivalent to *Jiva* in the terminology of Bhagavad Gita. Right knowledge is Self-realization by *Purusha*'s withdrawal from this false identification. As seen from the lake analogy, both good and bad *karma* impede the journey of *Jiva* towards its ultimate Self-realization. In various religions this realization is associated with Heaven, God, both, or neither. The Yoga Sutras prescribe ways to put an end to the false identification, one of the ways being devotion to God (*Ishvara*). Patanjali introduces the idea of God into Sankhya. *Ishvara* is a special kind of Purusha, untouched by ignorance and the products of ignorance, not subject to *karmas* or *samskaras* or the results of action.

grosser and grosser forms out of *Akasha*: plants, animals, humans, stars, and so on. At the end of the cycle, all contents of the universe melt into the *Akasha* again, and the next creation similarly proceeds out of this *Akasha*. Both *Akasha* and *Prana* are incorporated into *Mahat* (Swami Vivekananda). *Mahat* which is the Cosmic Mind, one may say, is the Cosmic Computer that stores memories and impressions as well as governs the many senses and limbs, in other words, the machinery of the Cosmos. Whatever happens or has occurred in the past is stored in *Mahat*, in a manner that we may back-up files onto a computer and place them away. Only when we open or access them, do we have knowledge of them. This is the same basic way that *Mahat* also works (Lingham 2013).

Parts of Chapter 3 (Vibhuti Pada) of Yoga Sutras are used by Alice Bailey as proof of existence of *Akashic* Records (Trine 2010). Bailey wrote in her book Light of the Soul on The Yoga Sutras of Patanjali – Book 3 (Bailey 1927): "The *Akashic* record is like an immense photographic film, registering all the desires and earth experiences of our planet. Those who perceive it will see pictured thereon: The life experiences of every human being since time began, the reactions to experience of the entire animal kingdom, the aggregation of the thought-forms of a karmic nature (based on desire) of every human unit throughout time."

Oliver was 'born that way': As said earlier, in all his experiences in the state of Samapatti, Oliver was aware of his own state of mind as well as that of his subject's, and was able to know which was his own and which was that of the subject. This led to him asking himself where this ability came from since he had not received any specific training in that regard. Oliver found from Yoga Sutras that there are only two ways to become established in Samadhi.

1. A lifetime of study and meditation with an accredited teacher, or
2. To be 'born that way'.

The Samapatti experiences of Oliver raise a significant point in relation to the retention of information after death. If one is born that way (established in that state of Samadhi), it means that the ability or tendency to get into Samadhi must be arising from the experience and skill acquired in an earlier life. That is to say, the Samadhi was a skill and a *samskara* that is retained at the level of *Mahat*.

Bevan Reid and etheric fields (Jacka 2011): In 1986, a colleague of Oliver, Bevan Reid, conducted experiments on mouse fibroblast cultures in a bovine solution as part of his cancer research. Although he did not work directly with the human energy field, his work does have interesting implications for the possibility of retaining human experiences in space. First, Reid found that cell cultures grown in the presence of a mass of 10kg of lead had a shorter life span that was the norm. Then after removing the lead from the laboratory space, he found that fresh cell cultures still died at this accelerated rate. This effect on fresh cell cultures lasted for weeks (Lasting of the effect could be due to radiation from lead still remaining the laboratory space.) During these experiments, Reid placed some glass slides coated with polystyrene some distance away from the cell cultures and allowed the slides to dry. An almost identical copy of the cells was produced on the plain polystyrene and illustrated action at a distance and the possibility of the transmission of biological data through a subtle field without any physical contact. Reid concluded that some force was coming through space producing these affects related to bacteria. Polystyrene coated slides had the image of a cell, exact in its detail to the extent that it even included the same staining as in the earlier cell cultures. (In the first experiment, cells were stained to produce enough contrast when viewed through the microscope.) Reid assumed that the staining agent caused some trauma to the cells (an experience/affect, which he called insult to the cell). Tiny vortices were found to have formed in the polystyrene as it dried. Reid thought that vortices appeared when form is imprinted on matter. In his experiments, he saw a continuous interaction between space and matter. He envisaged the outflow from matter to produce an exact copy of the form and that the inflow from the etheric into biological/living matter to carry instructions for the pattern of a growing structure.

5. Who is capable of knowing the retained information?

Purusha, the Self, the pure Consciousness is the seer. What is seen? The whole of nature, beginning with the mind, down to gross matter.

In Chapter 3, Patanjali describes a capability called *Samyama*, which is the inclusive term for three progressive states of attention: concentration, meditation, and absorption (*Samadhi*). Various psychic powers (called *siddhis*) are acquired and manifested by directing *Samyama* on specific objects, thoughts, or phenomena. For example, *Samyama* on the navel *chakra* yields knowledge of the body's constitution; *samyama* on the spiritual heart (*hrdaya*), the center of our being yields knowledge of the nature of consciousness[13] (Trine 2010). Some individuals may be endowed with *siddhis* by birth. When someone is born with a *siddhi*, it is because of the *samskaras*

---

[13]   In this chapter, Patanjali enumerates several possibilities and potential powers such as moving through *Akasha*, clairvoyance, and clairaudience. He says that the yogi acquires mastery of *Prakriti* in other words, control of Nature.

that someone developed in a previous birth. In this birth he is born, as it were, to enjoy the fruits of them.

After reading the Yoga Sutras of Patanjali, Oliver found a description of *Samadhi* (Samapatti being one kind of *Samadhi*), in Yoga Sutra 1.41. He also found that one enters this state when all fluctuations of the mind are brought under control. Sutra 1.41 says the following: The Yogi whose Vrttis (thoughts) have become powerless (controlled) obtains in the receiver, receiving, and received (the self, the mind and objects of perception), concentration and sameness, like the crystal (before different coloured objects.) What results from this constant meditation? In a previous aphorism Patanjali went into the various states of meditation, and how the first will be the gross, and the second the fine objects, and from them the advance is to still finer objects of meditation. Here the Yogi sees the three things, the receiver, the received, and the receiving, corresponding to the soul, the object, and the mind. There are three objects of meditation given us. First, the gross things: bodies, or material objects, second, fine things: the mind, and third, the egoism. By practice, the Yogi gets established in all these meditations. Whenever he meditates he can keep out all other thought; he becomes identified with that which he mediates upon; when he meditates he is like a piece of crystal before flowers; the crystal becomes almost identified with flowers. If the flower is red, the crystal looks red, or if the flower is blue, the crystal looks blue. In chapter 3 of Yoga Sutras, it is said that it is only in the beyond-sensory perception of *samadhi* that we see an object in the truth of its own nature, absolutely free from the distortions of our imagination. *Samadhi* is, in fact, much more than perception; it is direct knowledge.

One of Oliver's Samapatti experiences which provides an example of the above scenario is as follows: He had been called to the hospital bedside of his daughter who was in a coma, having rejected an earlier heart and lungs transplant. As he sat looking at her he went into a state of intense bliss, hardly the response one would expect from a father looking at his dying daughter. As in other Samapatti examples mentioned earlier, by meditating upon the state of mind of his daughter, Oliver, the seer became aware of the state of his subject'/ daughter's mind; the seer was also aware that the subject's mind was in that state but not Oliver's. Oliver is sure that he experienced her state of mind by merging his mind with hers because Oliver never experienced the same bliss when he remembered and reported that event to others later in life. She must have been in a state of bliss at that time; she might have been in an NDE since NDEs usually have feelings of love, joy, peace, and/or bliss. Moreover, since one aspect of *Samadhi* is absence of grief, its absence in the above situation is another indication of being in the Samadhi state. We may say that in this Samapatti experience, while the seer is *Purusha* (Oliver being in the state of *Purusha* because he is the conscious being), the object of knowledge, the state of bliss of his daughter in coma is in *Mahat*.

Yoga Sutra 4.1 says that psychic powers may be obtained either by birth, or by means of drugs, or by the power of words (blessings from others), or by the practice of austerities, or by *Samadhi*. Hence *Samadhi* is not the only way to know information that survives the bodily death of an individual. As an example, clairvoyant, Claire Barry who is also an astrologer, palmist and numerologist wrote about life after death, meaning consciousness after death, in her book Godlet (Barry 2016). A client, we shall call him Steven, sought help from Claire in understanding events in his personal life, specifically, to find out if there was any spiritual method for proving one way or another whether those close to him had been associated with him at other times. By reading Steven's astrological chart she could say that

195

indeed, some had been in similar relationships at another time and place. Steven flew to France to put Claire's astrological conclusions to test and began an odyssey covering the lives of this person and his extended family and acquaintances. Throughout Steven's journey, Claire gave him information about the culture, the landscape, and geography in such minute detail that he could find the exact place, and exact house he needed to reach.

6. Conclusion

"Does Consciousness End, Continue, Awaken, or Transform When the Body Dies?" is a question which, occupied the minds of prominent thinkers of all civilizations ever since ancient times. Interest in finding answers to this question continues even today as seen from the growing literature on reincarnation, NDEs, OBEs, and other paranormal phenomena. We have presented personal experiences of one of the authors (Oliver's), of a conscious but thoughtless state called Samapatti, as examples to support the view that consciousness is independent of the body. Oliver got into the Samapatti state whenever he focussed his mind on a human or animal subject; in that state, his mind became still and then he became aware of some physical or psychological conditions of the subject. Hence these experiences showed one can be conscious without the usual in-and-out thought flow and be aware of something external to one's own body and mind without any physical or sensory connection. Thus, they show that consciousness is not produced by the body or brain. If consciousness is independent of the body, it follows that consciousness does not end, nor awaken, nor transform with bodily death but continues unaffected.

According to Hindu Philosophy, consciousness (if interpreted as the ability to know) is not created by the body or brain and is always there everywhere unaffected by the birth, life, and death of any individual. This philosophy also says that the mind which is an accumulation of the information content of all conscious experiences in one's life together with any unconscious thoughts and desires, survives physical death as well; mind is not conscious by itself but it is the object of knowing, in other words, object of consciousness. Interestingly, today's research in NDE and OBE seems to validate Hindu philosophy's propositions that mind and consciousness are not necessarily dependent of the state of the body or brain. Many Eastern philosophies believe in the existence of a soul in each living being which does not end with the death of the body but can take another life; the soul may carry with it some of the surviving mind into the new life. Again, today's research in reincarnation seems to support Hindu philosophy's view that knowledge and influences of experiences in past lives may be carried over into a new life. The observation that some are able to report NDEs, OBEs, past-life experiences, etc. shows that the information content of such experiences must have been retained somewhere that is not a physical medium until its reporter is able to find it and report it, because the information is not known to others by normal (sensory and material) means. Patanjali yoga Sutras seem to have considered the question of where this information is stored.

7. References

Bailey Alice. The Light of the Soul: Its Science and Effect: a Paraphrase of the Yoga Sutras of Patañjali. Lucis, 1927. http://www.think-downloads.com/download/Spiritual/Light%20of%20the%20Soul%20-%20Alice%20Bailey.pdf

Barry Claire. Godlet- From the Other Side of the Mirror. S.A. Design & Print. Port Elliot South Australia 5212. 2016.

Carr Bernard. Ian Stevenson and His Impact on Foreign Shores. Journal of Scientific Exploration 2008; 22(1): 87–92.

Greyson Bruce. Cosmological Implications of Near-Death Experiences. Journal of Cosmology, 2011; 14.

Hari S. How Vedanta Explains Conscious Subjective Experience. Journal of Consciousness Exploration & Research 2015; 6(4): 209 – 221.

Hari S, Oliver Alan J. Explaining Samapatti & Knowing without Mind by Vedanta.

Journal of Consciousness Exploration & Research 2015; 6(12):1001 -1014.

Hari S. Psychons could be zero-energy tachyons. NeuroQuantology 2008, 6 (2):152.

Hari S. Mind and Tachyons: How Tachyon Changes Quantum Potential and Brain Creates Mind.

NeuroQuantology 2011, 9(2): 255.

Hari S. Mind and Tachyons: Quantum interactive dualism - Libet's causal anomalies.

NeuroQuantology 2014, 12(2); 247.

Hari S. Mind and tachyons in six-dimensional special relativity. NeuroQuantology 2016, 14(1):

94-105.

Jacka Judy. The Human Energy Field. ACNEM Journal December 2011; 30 (3): 5.

Kihlstrom John F. The rediscovery of the unconscious. In H. Morowitz& J. L. Singer (Eds.). The mind, the brain, and complex adaptive systems. Addison-Wesley Publishing Co, Inc. 1994; 123-143. http://socrates.berkeley.edu/~kihlstrm/rediscovery.htm

Lingham. Durgadas (Rodney). Secrets of the *Mahat*: The Cosmic Intelligence. Lulu.com. 2013.

Mormann Florian and Koch Christof. Scholarpedia 2007; 2(12):1740.

Mukherjee B D. The Essence of Bhagavad Gita. Academic Publishers 2002; Kolkata.

Smythies John R. Consciousness and Higher Dimensions of Space. Journal of Consciousness Studies 2012; **19**(11–12): 224–232.

Stevenson Ian. Twenty Cases Suggestive of Reincarnation. University of Virginia Press, 1980.

https://med.virginia.edu/perceptual-studies/

Swami Prabhvaananda and Christopher Isherwood. The Yoga Aphorisms of Patanjai. Sri Ramakrishna Math, Mylapore, Chennai, India. http://www.estudantedavedanta.net/Yoga-Aphorisms-of-Patanjali.pdf

Swami Shravananda. Kenopanishad. The Ramakrishna Math, Mylapore, Madras 1920.

Swami Vivekananda. Raja Yoga. Kegan Paul, Trench Trubner & Company, Limited, 1893. http://hinduonline.co/DigitalLibrary/SmallBooks/PatanjaliYogaSutraSwamiVivekanandaSanEng.pdf

Swami Vivekananda. The Vedanta Philosophy. The Vivekanada Foundation. http://web.csulb.edu/~wweinste/vedanta.html

http://shardsofconsciousness.com/user/sites/shardsofconsciousness.com/files/ebooks/RajaYoga_Vivekananda.pdf

Trine Cheryl. The New Akashic Records: Knowing, Healing& Spiritual Practice. Essential Knowing Press. 2010.